TO LOVE AGAIN

Intimate Relationships After 60

TO LOVE AGAIN

Intimate Relationships After 60

Florence Mason

Illustrations by Glenn Bernhardt

GATEWAY BOOKS

San Francisco

Printed in the United States of America

Gateway Books
San Francisco

Library of Congress Cataloging-in-Publication Data

Mason, Florence.
   To love again.

   1. Aged—United States—Miscellanea. 2. Intimacy
(Psychology)—Miscellanea. 3. Remarriage—United States
—Micellanea. I. Title.
HQ1064.U5M385 1989   305.26'0973   89–1463
ISBN 0-933469-05-5

12 11 10 9 8 7 6 5 4 3 2 1

ACKNOWLEDGEMENTS

There's a small group of wonderful human beings who get star billing in my life and under the above heading: my four offspring. Carol Anne, Polly, Kathy and George (who wields an incisive blue pencil) each contributed in her or his individual, unique and often practical way to the making of this book. Nothing was more important than their lovingkindness, which, after all, is what this book is about — in a different context.

The other group deserving thanks and praise beyond measure: the 65 men and women who opened their lives, their minds and their hearts to this interviewer. In almost every case, the interviewee said, "Why are you interviewing me? I'm not special; I have nothing important to tell you." And in every case that person was wrong; each and every one was special and had something important to say, as you will see. It's their book.

Glenn Bernhardt's artistry rounds it out. He has a special gift for illustrating the spirit behind the written words, and our collaboration has been a joy.

The men in my life, over the years, will know who they are and how they contributed to the making of this book. Perhaps it is unfortunate that they, like those interviewed, must remain anonymous. Perhaps not.

The publishers of this book — Gateway Books, in the persons of Donald and Judith Merwin — brought harmony to our business association. Their openness to my concept of the book, and their ability to bring it to life, have been of immeasurable value.

Florence Mason
Carmel, California

For Carol Anne, Polly, George and Kathy
and the one man.

CONTENTS

INTRODUCTION

"Grow old along with me!
The best is yet to be,
The last of life, for which the first was made."
Rabbi Ben Ezra by Robert Browning

What's it like, being in love when you are over 60? Many of the voices in this book echo Browning's words. Others would rather grow old alone; they believe the best has already been. None would take issue with the last line, however. As an inscription on the National Archives Building in Washington, D.C. reads: "The heritage of the past is the seed that brings forth the harvest of the future." This book is about that harvest as it affects intimate relationships.

The book evolved out of my own experience in such a relationship and subsequently, my curiosity about how it is for others over 60 who are single, or recently married. I asked myself, then others: why is "elderlove" so special...especially joyous, especially painful? And: do I want to be involved again — do I want to love again?

While this book is not about statistics, there are statistics that speak to its importance, and to its importance *now:*

- In 1986, 12.1 percent of Americans were 65 or older, compared to 11 percent in 1980.
- That 65-and-older population has grown twice as fast

as the rest of our population since the early 1960s. By the year 2030, one-fifth of all Americans will be over 65.

• There are 10.8 million widows and almost 2 million widowers in the United States today — 7.2 percent of the adult population. An estimated 56,000 people past age 65 get married every year and 10,000 get divorced.

• For the first time in history, there are more Americans over 65 than there are teenagers.

• When the baby boom reappears as the golden oldies boom, the full social and financial impact will be felt. Early in the next century, nearly two-thirds of the federal budget will be claimed by the over-65's.

I'm often asked how I found the people who contribute to those statistics and whose words grace this book. Friends were first, as I reached out to share my own experience and to find out if it was unique. And then it was friends of friends; each person I interviewed knew someone else I should approach. I also followed listings of marriage licenses in the local paper and, when at least one of the newlyweds was over 60, I attempted — often successfully — to locate them. I also put in the local paper what I hoped would be an enticing ad, but that garnered only two replies, neither promising. The best leads, both in my home territory and during a three-month sojourn in Vermont, continued to be friends and acquaintances.

The people who speak in this book come from various walks of life and I learned that thoughts and feelings about intimate relationships are not defined by education, color or sexual orientation. We all bring a lifetime of experience with families and work and money that has established points of view, standards, opinions, prejudices; we bring an education in living.

The other side of the coin is that each of us has a limited future to look forward to. Some, more years than others in these days of medical progress and medical miracles. But still, limited.

One way in which I found that limitation having an effect is in the standards that men and women over 60 have — standards they impose on the opposite sex. For the lonely or frightened or bored or insecure, those standards may be lower. For the hurt and therefore wary, the comfortable or the secure, standards may be higher than they were when they were in their marrying 20s or 30s. One divorced man of 60 told me that his standards are higher now "because the longer I live the more women there are!"

All but one of my interviewees insisted on anonymity, often before they would agree to be interviewed. I was happy to comply. Names, places, and some other distinquishing details have been changed. But except for those changes, every quotation in this book is written just as it was spoken. These words do not come together into any sort of consensus; their differences and contrasts are what brought this book to life.

In the process of putting these words together I experimented with other formats such as fiction, or creating one couple to act as narrators. But nothing improved on the basic formula of letting these men and women speak for themselves. Along the way I was tempted to take a stand for or against getting involved in intimate relationships (defined here as friendship, love, affairs, marriage — all the different ways in which older men and older women do relate intimately). You will have to judge for yourselves how successful I was in resisting that temptation.

While this is not essentially a "how-to" book, it is inevitable that some useful knowledge will find its way out of the words that "tell it like it is."

So: get ready to meet some wonderful people within these pages. You may recognize a friend, a relative, a client, a neighbor, or... yourself.

Florence Mason
Carmel, CA
1989

I

WILL YOU, WON'T YOU, WILL YOU, WON'T YOU, WILL YOU JOIN THE DANCE?

The Lobster Quadrille by Lewis Carroll

"Grow old along with me!"
    No! It's too late.
"The best is yet to be."
    No! My memories are better.
"The last of life, for which the first was made."
    No way! Romance is for youth. Forget it!

In the September — or December — of my life, do I want to be involved in an intimate relationship? Is such an emotional investment worth the risks? Each of us must answer this question for himself or herself.

I set out to find my own answer. Along the way I became involved in the lives and personal quests of 64 men and women — some single, some recently married; each, like me, at least 60 years old. From all the rationalizations, all the ambivalences expressed in our discussions, a chorus emerged. It soars like the last movement of Beethoven's Ninth Symphony, celebrating togetherness and separateness with equal fervor. Listen.

I'LL LIVE ALONE

I don't need anyone.

People would think I'm silly.

I'm out of practice.

He might drop dead.

I might lose her. I couldn't go through that again.

It's too much trouble.

I might have to move.

He might get sick.

She might break her hip.

I'd have to give up what I have for the unknown.

I'LL GO FOR IT

It's my last chance.

I hate to eat alone.

He would protect me.

I'd have someone to talk to.

I'd have a reason to put on a clean shirt.

I wouldn't ever have to worry about money again.

I would have someone to give things to.

I could stop looking.

I would recognize the face on the other pillow

    when I wake up.

Those eager to be involved use one word more often than any other. Is it *love? sex? security?* No, it's *companionship.*

"What am I coming home to? Nothing, no one. Without *companionship*, I'm not living. I'm merely existing."

"Everything just matters more when you're old. At the same time, *companions* are harder to come by; there's no one to share the joys and sorrows with."

"Even as a youngster, I was unhappy alone. I need *companionship* — someone for sharing, to talk with, to agree or disagree with. I dread old age, alone."

If this book had been written 20 years ago, it might have begun and ended with these paeans to companionship. Today, companionship is the common denominator in more diverse and intimate relationships between older men and women. We seniors have as many different points of view about these relationships as we have pages in our photo albums.

♂ *"I'm having a ball, with no strings attached. Make that no apron strings."*

"I NEED...SOMEONE FOR SHARING"

♀ *"I'm beyond romance. But I like having someone special —
someone to care about me, to think about me in practical
ways."*

♂ *"Why get involved now? I can be with women when I want
to be, but I don't have to be responsible for them. I'm
comfortable living alone."*

♀ *"Being single isn't so bad. I'm building a good life with both
male and female friends. I've had enough change for a while."*

♀ *"When I think about marriage, all I can envision is work —
housework."*

♂ *"The ads say you* can *have it all, and that's what I want —
everything that an intimate relationship can bring to my life.
I'd even marry again, if I had to."*

❋❋❋

THREE FRIENDS ARGUE ABOUT MARRIAGE, ONE FORM OF INTIMACY

"I enjoy the sharing we have, the love, but I'm not sure
I want to give up any more of my privacy."

"Sharing and a healthy respect for privacy aren't
mutually exclusive! Look at what you get with marriage:
a good chance to have someone to grow old with, to
share friends and memories and walks in the rain."

"Nowadays, you don't have to be married to have all
that!"

OTHERS FIND THEIR OWN PLACES ALONG THAT CONTINUUM: TO BE OR NOT BE MARRIED

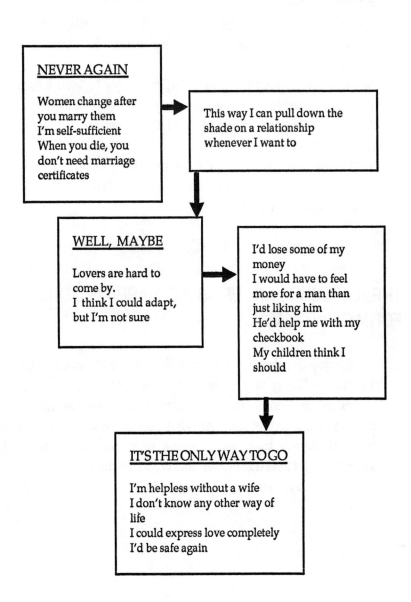

NEVER AGAIN

Women change after
you marry them
I'm self-sufficient
When you die, you
don't need marriage
certificates

This way I can pull down the
shade on a relationship
whenever I want to

WELL, MAYBE

Lovers are hard to
come by.
I think I could adapt,
but I'm not sure

I'd lose some of my
money
I would have to feel
more for a man than
just liking him
He'd help me with my
checkbook
My children think I
should

IT'S THE ONLY WAY TO GO

I'm helpless without a wife
I don't know any other way of
life
I could express love completely
I'd be safe again

The woman who said she wants marriage because she would be safe again knew a 65-year-old woman who had been robbed, beaten and raped in her home. She sent me an article that said violent crimes against the elderly increased from 139,000 in 1979 to 195,000 in 1981, the last year for which figures were available.

This runs counter to figures showing that violent crimes in general have declined nationally. No doubt the increase is at least partly due to increased numbers of elderly. But is it also because more of us are living alone? Many of us would find it easy to substitute the risks of marriage for the risks of violence.

BUT THE RISKS OF MARRIAGE CHANGE — INTENSIFY — WITH TIME

A petite seventy-year-old looks over the group waiting for the bus at the senior center. Beneath Jane's calm exterior is the mind and spirit of a huntress.

She quickly sorts the men into "possibles" and "not possibles." And the women? Competitors all! Her glance stops briefly at one man, Alan, definitely a "possible." If she can arrange it, she will sit next to him on the bus.

Alan has his own plans.

Although surrounded by four or five women before boarding the bus for a day in San Francisco, he, too, had managed to survey the entire group. He has seen Jane before — at the center — and likes the look of her. So he manages to get behind her as the passsengers line up to board the bus, then lowers his bulk into the seat next to hers.

This is exactly what Jane wanted. Why, then, does she turn away from Alan to gaze through the window? All the way to San Francisco, she sees him only as a wavering reflection.

I asked Jane about this several weeks after the bus trip. "I was so lonely," she said, "and at the same time, so afraid."

"Lonely" I could understand. Jane had been married to her college sweetheart for 35 years; he died three years ago, and their two children live on the East coast. But "afraid"?

"I can't see myself starting over and building all those blocks again," Jane explained. "What if I made a mistake? There isn't enough time to correct it. And what would the children say; how would they get along with him? What would he think about my body when he saw it every day? I don't even like it myself. Why, no one has seen me without my eyebrows for years! And what if I got sick — or he did? What if I became a widow — again?"

Jane laughed. "At my age, time is the enemy. And I know a lot of my desire is in my head. I don't even know if I'd have the energy for an intimate relationship, if it did come my way."

SOME KNOW THE ANSWER — FOR THEMSELVES

♂ *"I know a guy who has one woman for tennis, one who's a good cook, and one who travels well! Me? Nothing about living alone bothers me. I've got two brothers, both helpless without their wives. But I've been divorced a long time and I'm better off than they are, better off then I've ever been. I'm content — with my house, the beach, my consulting work, my dogs. I'd never give up the present for something unknown."*

♂ *"My new marriage is splendid! I have the wonderful companionship of a woman, and great sex. And also, because she learned to like being by herself when she was alone for so many years, there are times when I can go home after a game of tennis and settle down outside with a book and a drink. She doesn't even demand — as my first wife did — that I call home if I decide to stay on for another set.* It's a lifetime of experience that makes all this possible."

♀ *"It's ironic. I spent five years figuring out how much of me was me and how much had been my husband and to get my career and everything else the way I wanted them. I was doing so well! It was like being on a diet; I had learned to live with different satisfactions — different foods. And then I met Ed. It was like suddenly being allowed to eat goodies again. It's great! Would it be so great if I had met Ed five years ago, right after my husband died?* I don't think so; this is the best time of my life."

II

"BE COMFORT TO MY AGE"

As You Like It by William Shakespeare

SOME MYTHS ABOUT US OLD FOLKS (INCLUDING THAT WE'RE ALL PRETTY MUCH ALIKE)

- Most of us are "senile" (whatever that means)
- Most of us have no interest in, or capacity for, sexual relationships
- Most of us are set in our ways and are unable to change or learn new things
- All of us are bored, and boring

Sometimes we give in to these myths ourselves:

"If I had just met you when we were young...."

"I make forays into an active life from time to time, but then I slip back into my old routine — like a well-worn road map slipping back into its folds."

The *truth* is that many older men and women are bright, sexy, interesting, eager to embrace new ideas. Of course some of us are boring, inflexible, sexually inactive — but so are some 40-year-olds. And we are as different, one from another, as the members of any other group in society.

Researchers have found that men and women who reach their late sixties can look forward to 10 or more years of active, independent life. To my own knowledge, many of us are still looking forward in our seventies, eighties and nineties.

The media do let us know that there are some non-senile, active senior citizens out there who accept challenges to learn and do new things, to be agents of change: Ronald Reagan, Leonard Bernstein, Julia Child, the late Winston Churchill, Grandma Moses and Georgia O'Keeffe. These people are treated as remarkable. The truth is, you can find their counterparts in Anytown:

— the 66-year-old woman who has just begun a new career as an actress in community theatre
— the men and women vying for top prizes in the senior brackets of tennis tournaments
— the vast numbers flocking to Elderhostel programs, summer alumni "colleges" and study tours
— members of city councils and commissions who are over 70, over 80, and still feisty

And you can hear them Everywhere:

"In those first few weeks, we acted like two young people. We had 130 years between us!"

"...WE ACTED LIKE TWO YOUNG PEOPLE."

"It's comfortable with an old broad like you. I don't have to explain who Ronald Coleman is — or anything like that." (Walter Matthau to Glenda Jackson in "House Calls")

A 40-year-old woman to her mother, who is 70: "I love your letters; they're always so exciting. The kids ask expectantly: 'What's Grandma up to now?'"

IT'S THE TRUTH

• Our bodies *aren't* what they used to be. We know it, and others remind us.

Women in their sixties and seventies grew up in a society that openly emphasized the value of physical appearance. Now, faced with competition from younger women for the few "older" men there are, many of us look at our bodies with distaste or, at least, concern; some with the saving grace of humor, like these women.

"Oh sure, I know my body has changed. Some parts look good: things become thin, like my arms and legs. But other parts...my stomach look like a built-in snack tray!"

"I was looking for an apartment, and answered an ad. The owner asked me how old I was. Immediately defensive, I hedged, 'I'm in my sixties.' (Well, I am 69.) The apartment owner said: 'Oh, that won't do; there are stairs up to this apartment.' Having just come in from my daily two-mile jog on the beach, I was ready to take her on. But I decided it wasn't worth the trouble."

"I saw an ad on TV for a denture adhesive. The woman, who looks about 65, is asked about her most embarrassing moment. She says, 'It was at my wedding last year! When I started to say "I do," my dentures nearly fell out.' Of course she bought the new adhesive, and that solved all her problems."

What men fear most, as they age, is the loss of pep and energy. However, increasing numbers are also turning to cosmetologists and plastic surgeons and their age-defying techniques. A recent market survey showed that 60 percent of the men interviewed found wrinkles even more depressing than gray hair or baldness.

IT'S THE TRUTH

• The older we are, the more important physical fitness is in achieving that independent, active life.

And if we're fit, how do we use our energy and resources? How much of these do we expend trying to beat the clock? As Elizabeth Kubler-Ross said in a televised interview: "We have not only taken the dignity out of dying, we have taken it out of living. Aging is (regarded as) a disgrace; we spend millions taking out those beautiful wrinkles."

Or as Henry Fonda put it so beautifully to Myrna Loy in "Summer Solstice": "It took me a long time to put those wrinkles there — let me enjoy them."

IT'S THE TRUTH

• Older men generally prefer to date, live with, and/or marry younger women.

"This is not a new story. To draw a parallel with early Greece: in the Greek tragedies, it is the young women and virginal goddesses who are helpful to men. Meanwhile, the mature goddesses tend to be portrayed as jealous, vindictive and destructive." (Pierre Mornell, M.D. *Passive Men, Wild Women*)

Dr. Mornell goes back to antiquity to prove his point that the real attraction of older men to younger women may have very little to do with *sex*; it has more to do with "a man's desire to find a woman who will accept him as he is...someone who will provide that personal rooting section for his uniqueness and accomplishments...He views the younger woman as less of a threat."

Most of the single men I interviewed (all over 60) seemed genuinely surprised to hear themselves admit a preference for younger women. They often started off with mild protests:

"Even at my age (65), people think you are a dirty old man when you are with someone younger. That's not how it is with us. My friend is 42. She is incredibly intelligent, has a marvelous sense of humor. And I'm not your typical macho man — I hadn't deliberately gone out looking for a younger woman."

"I tend to date rather physical types and that usually means younger. Women my own age don't fit into my jogging, hiking and so on. Younger women have more zest for life, the things I want."

"I have seen women well past 50 who are knockouts. But they're usually involved with someone else."

But some are forthright:

"Yes, age is usually a factor. The women I have felt most at home with have been somewhat younger, about 10 years."

"My pattern is women between 30 and 40. Don't ask me why."

And some hedge their bets:

"I don't really enjoy 'young' women. There are such differences in taste, music, conversation. I don't consciously set any limits on chronological age but I do enjoy talk that has some depth. Even so, I haven't dated women *older* than I. I've always associated with younger people because I have been a teacher."

"Do I prefer younger women? Sure, why not! But my better sense says that isn't for me. It would be o.k. for a day or so but if I'm looking for a companion, I'm not looking for a younger woman."

"If it's a long-lasting relationship, an age difference begins to stretch. And it could be a sex problem; I might reach a point where I am incapable."

"When I was single, I wasn't interested in younger women because they wouldn't be interested in me."

"I might prefer a younger woman, but I have too much common sense."

"I met a divorcee who was only two years older than my daughter. She asked me for advice about some business problems and I took her out for dinner. Later, she said she fell in love with me then. My feelings developed quickly, too. But for me it was teen-age stuff, a ridiculous relationship. My daughter was shocked. My new friend told me that I intrigued her. I realized that I felt the way I did about her because of her response to me. I guess that was partly physical; even the touching was great." He concluded that he felt both guilty and foolish about the relationship. He broke it up after six months.

OLDER WOMEN RESPOND, WITH VIGOR

"Damn! Ever since I turned 60, I have felt that I am invisible."

"A man thinks if he can attract a younger woman it says something about his virility. Why don't they think about the person? If I can hold my own playing tennis with you, walk your dog with you, go salmon fishing, stay up late, enjoy sex, get up early...what difference does it make what the calendar says about how old I am? Don't tell me your ego needs don't have anything to do with it!"

"I'm 70, he is 62. I run circles around him."

"A few years ago I was dating an older man and he kept bringing up age as a problem for us. I was 45, he was 60 or something, so naturally I assumed he meant that he was too old for me. I kept trying to reassure him. Well, it turned out that he meant I was too old for him! Later, he married a woman of 30."

"Even sensible Dr. Spock, who is 82, is married to a woman of 41. And he admits to having problems with a 19-year-old stepdaughter."

"It's not fair! There aren't enough older men to go around as it is!"

To which one man countered:

"What's fairness got to do with it? I grew up in a fairly Puritan atmosphere, and I was married for a long time. A part of my life is unsatisfied. I like the 'new morality' and just wish it had been that way when I was young. If I have the energy for younger women now, why not?"

IT'S THE TRUTH

• Many older women are not interested in men who are much older than they are, *or act that way.*

"When I'm asked out by a man who is the same age, I think, 'Oh, how old!' But I realize I may be comparing him with my husband at the age he was when he died. Whatever the reason, men my age do look too old for me."

"I can understand that men want to press younger flesh, as it were. Younger women are generally more esthetically pleasing. That certainly makes it tough. The only man I could be 'younger' to would be someone in his seventies. I don't know many men that age *I'd* be attracted to!"

"My daughter-in-law wanted to match me with her father. He's a sweet little man but he doesn't have any aspirations left and I couldn't stand that. He's only 60, but he acts much older."

❋❋❋

A woman in her eighties told me about an attentive 'older' male in the retirement home where she lives. "It's too late," she said. "I've given up on getting a man. What would I do with one?" "Put him in a rocking chair by your side, " I offered. The woman replied: "I'd like that. But I'm afraid he'd never get up again!"

❋❋❋

ARE "MAY-OCTOBER" ALLIANCES A SOLUTION FOR WOMEN? Some Women Don't Think So.

"I heard a 60-year old man complain because much younger men are now taking women in their fifties and sixties off the market. That'll be the day! *I keep hearing about it, but I've never seen it.*"

"I used to go out with a man 10 years younger. *But it was too strenuous.* He led the pack when we went out with the Sierra Club, and I brought up the rear."

"I know one man who flipped out of his age bracket to an older woman. *Is it because older women don't frighten younger men?*"

"I'm younger looking, but that doesn't give me a license to take on a younger man. I like looking up to a man. *I don't want to be in charge.*"

"I have good relationships with younger men, but I wouldn't date them. Late sixties are o.k. for me now that I'm in my seventies. But who's available? *'Age hath its privileges' doesn't apply to dating.*"

"The double standard persists. The picture of a 65-year-old man with a young blond is acceptable, common. But if it's a 65-year-old woman with a younger man, *'He must be after her money.'*"

ARE THERE ANSWERS?   Well, Some Of Us Think So.

♂ *"I only date women of my generation. But I am with younger people as often as possible. I love their frankness and vitality."*

♀ *"He is 11 years older...is that a problem? No, he's so active. The differences between us would be the same regardless of age."*

♀ *"My friend is 10 years younger. His being a nice person is more important than age. My husband was older, and I like older men too. Any man!"*

♂ *"The age difference between us — I'm 12 years younger — hasn't been a problem, except when it comes to sports. I can't keep up with her tennis, and she doesn't play golf. So we go our separate ways — on Saturdays."*

♀ *"Age doesn't mean very much; the point is how you act. The man I'm seeing now is 15 years older; it's great."*

♂ *"It isn't any different for gays. I try not to be too nostalgic with my younger friend."*

♀ *"Age? What's that?"*

III

GETTING STARTED

IT'S A FACT:

- More than 11 percent of all Americans are 65 or older.
- There are five widows for every widower in the United States (10.8 million vs. 2 million); together they make up 7.2 percent of the adult population.
- In three percent of all the weddings in this country, at least one person is over 65.

If some of us decide to go for it, to push toward an intimate relationship, perhaps even to join that small but significant three percent marrying after 65, where do we start?

One possibility: a dating service. But you won't find equal rights for women there. All the "introduction" or dating agencies I contacted reported an abundance of female applicants and a relative scarcity of men. (I even heard about one in Shanghai that specializes in matchmaking for seniors. It received 800 inquiries in its first month of business. But few introductions were made. Why? Females responding to the agency's ad outnumbered males five to one.)

There is some indication that this gap narrows among older participants, perhaps because older men tire of the chase and are looking for easier avenues. One agency owner suggested that older women tend to be less aggressive than their younger sisters when it comes to seeking a relationship; they may settle comfortably into single domesticity.

What other ways are there? I asked around.

DIFFERENT WOMEN, DIFFERENT ANSWERS

Myra S. "How do I meet men? At small parties, where you can talk more easily to one or two. Through my volunteer work. I've also had some fine encounters while walking my dogs. "

Jane P. " I went to a college reunion, met a man who had recently been divorced, and spent the weekend with him. Until that time I hadn't dated anyone since my husband died, two years before. I certainly wasn't expecting what happened at the reunion; I hadn't seen that man for 36 years! But he was good for me that weekend, and I'll see him again."

Helen M. "We started working together professionally, after having known each other casually for years. I was never going to get married again! And yet it was easy to say 'yes' to him because it was all very comfortable by then."

Pat S. "Several months ago I was at a weekend conference in another city. Late one night there was a party in the room next door that had gotten pretty noisy. I knocked on the door and an attractive white-haired man opened it. He looked amused, and no wonder: here was this vision in a bathrobe, with curlers in her hair and cream on her face. I asked him if the party could quiet down. He apologized. The next morning, when we met in the dining room, he didn't even recognize me. We had breakfast together, and that was the beginning. We often laugh about the way we met. I had gone to the conference hoping to meet someone there, but I wasn't thinking about that when I knocked on his door — only about getting my beauty sleep!"

WHAT ABOUT THE MEN?

Frank T. " I go to see widows and offer to help them sort things out. Friends invite me to dinner, just to meet someone new. I like some of the women and with others it's take-'em-or-leave-'em. I meet women playing tennis and golf. One lady came by to see my house, which is for sale; she became a fourth for bridge."

Bob M. "I met Helen at a garage sale. Weeks passed before I realized I was looking forward to seeing her each Saturday, not just to finding a lost Picasso! Finally, one morning, we began a mock argument over who had claimed some pewter dishes first. She let me win; I invited her to lunch. Now we are going to garage sales together. We need lots of things for our new home."

Howard L. "Jean read some of her poetry at a writer's seminar I attended. It was a very emotional moment for me. Her poetry was fantastic, soaring. And she was beautiful. After the reading we talked, and we listened to each other. My life changed that day. I had been looking, but had recently decided it was all over; romance hadn't worked out for me — why bother? I didn't have to ask 'why bother?' when I met Jean."

Cecil P. "I'm a very skilled widower. And it's easy — for men. There are eight or 12 eligible women in this town for every single man, and I just let them know I'm available. One 80-year-old calls me early in the morning to make a date. I warned her about running into some of my other lady friends if she comes by too early."

NO ONE HANDS OUT GUARANTEES!

♀ *"There was a man who came to my office frequently and always stopped to talk to me. I knew he wasn't married. I thought of asking him to dinner, but I didn't do it for months. Then a friend said, 'Why not? What's the worst thing that can happen?' and so I did. The man said, 'I'm already in a relationship.' I felt completely rejected; he wasn't even nice about it. I won't try that again."*

♂ *"Lots of people use groups, even Alcoholics Anonymous, to meet people. But when I was involved in a volunteer group and ran up against several women who were there just to meet men, the group lost its value for me. I'd like to tell women not to have false hopes, to be realistic. If you are out trapping, don't walk too far!"*

"...IT'S EASY... FOR MEN..."

♂ *"I thought I'd never find anyone. I did all the groups, like Parents Without Partners, and all the right parties. I even went to a Spanish class, looking for someone who might like to go to Mexico with me. But one day I woke up in that class and thought, 'What am I doing here? I don't really want to learn Spanish.' And I didn't go back. I'm still looking."*

♀ *"I have often been bored. One man, recently divorced, invited me out to dinner. It was a stale conversation. Then the women in his neighborhood rallied around him and told him he would have to sharpen up if he wanted to get started dating again. He graduated from baggy pants to trim ones and to a red jacket. He learned to converse and to cook, give parties. Then his wife returned and they remarried!"*

DON'T PUSH! OR WHATEVER HAPPENED TO WOMEN'S LIB?

♂ *"Women should never pursue a man on the telephone. And a woman should never say she is lonely, because that drives a man up the wall."*

♂ *"A woman called me. She sounded as scared as I was. We talked on the phone every few days for several weeks before we actually met. Then I drove the 50 miles to her home to take her to dinner. 'Consider yourself being courted,' I said."*

♂ *"I had a number of 'girl friends' after my wife died, but none rang my bell. Then this kook came along. She was the first woman who wasn't overly nice to me, or real pushy, who didn't make a pest of herself. It was just a coming together of congenial people."*

♂ *"I'm fair game now. But I hate to be pursued; I want to be the one to take the initiative. I'm pursued by women, even some in their thirties. The ones I see, the ones I like, I have met through my business. One thing leads to another..."*

♀ *"Right after my husband died, a mutual friend told me she had a man for me, but it was nine months before I was ready to meet him. It 'took' immediately; away we went! He told me later that if I had phoned him, he wouldn't have responded. But this way was o.k."*

What happened is that women's lib hasn't rubbed off on many men who are over 60.

A larger percentage of older women have embraced and prize their freedom from stereotypical roles in relation to men, but even here the old ways sometimes die hard.

♀ *"I don't go to senior activities, because they are about 70 percent women, 30 percent men. Many of the women are very aggressive and predatory, but not me. I have never had to go after a man in my life and I'm not about to start now."*

GETTING STARTED MEANS TAKING CHANCES (and we do)

♀ *"Every time a man becomes a widower, it's a lottery to see who gets to him first! I have my running shoes on."*
♀ *"Younger friends said, 'Get out and meet people.' So I kicked myself out the door."*

♂ *"After my wife died, a friend of hers brought over a fruit cake for me. I invited her for a ride...now we've been married two years."*

♂ *"My son has thrown me in the back of a car with a blind date once in a while."*

♂ *"My first date, when I was young, was in a horse-and-buggy. I met the woman I am seeing now in a health spa."*

♀ *"My grandson said, 'Go for it, Grandma!' So I went for it."*

"Dearly beloved, we are gathered together..."

Thus begins a marriage ceremony. The path toward this
moment of unity is rocky, as is the path that leads into the
future. What special problems, what special joys will older
men and women encounter along that path? We are about to
find out.

> *"Then welcome each rebuff*
> *That turns earth's smoothness rough,*
> *Each sting that bids nor sit nor stand, but go!*
> *Be our joys three parts pain!*
> *Strive, and hold cheap the strain;*
> *Learn, nor account the pang; dare,*
>   *never grudge the throe!"*

Rabbi Ben Ezra by Robert Browning

IV

GOING FOR IT: WE ARE GATHERED TOGETHER

"You can't do that!"

"Why can't I?"

"Because — well, because it wouldn't look right. You and Ted aren't married."

"But times have changed."

"They haven't changed that much. Some things still matter. Or they should. If you want to go on a cruise with him, at least get adjoining rooms..."

Not an unusual conversation between a mother and daughter — right?

But the first speaker is in fact the *daughter*, who is scolding her mother for flaunting her relationship with a 68-year-old lover.

The mother says: "My daughter had a disastrous marriage, which is why she is afraid of my 'getting romantic at this age.'"

Then there's the 62-year old man whose son said, "Why don't you just go and live with her?" The man's mother, 92, said, "I wish you'd marry her first."

And the 75-year-old woman who said to her lover, 70: "How do we explain you to my grandchildren?"

We older men and women are not alone when we worry about the risks of intimate relationships; the voices of our families and friends join in with gusto. "Talk about extended families!" one woman said. "Between us, we have nine children and step-children, also seven sisters and brothers. And my husband's parents are still living, in their nineties; he feels responsible for them."

The result may be harmony — or discord.

***

HARMONY

♀ *"His sons were wonderful. All three had hair cuts for our wedding. They even wore tuxes!"*

♂ *"We wouldn't have gotten married if it hadn't worked out for our families, too. Or at least not until problems were solved. My children have come around beautifully because of my new wife's concern and sensitivity. Her sons just wanted her to be sure, because she had said she didn't want to get married again. My kids said she would take care of me! All our children and three grandchildren were at our wedding. My oldest grandchild said, 'It's just like a fairy tale.'"*

"HOW DO WE EXPLAIN YOU TO MY GRANDCHILDREN?"

♂ *"My second wife is thoughtful about everyone in my family. She even went to see my first wife's mother; they got along famously."*

♂ *"None of the four children we have between us has influenced the course of our relationship. We have sworn fidelity to one another and will allow no one to sway our course."*

♀ *"My son called to ask how our dates were. He urged me to be more aggressive. I'm trying!"*

DISCORD

♂ *"It has been hard for Ethel to give up her dependence on her oldest daughter, who has been her sounding board since her husband died — years ago."*

♂ *"I'm concerned that younger women, whom I prefer, may be encumbered by children."*

♀ *"My son, whom I've been helping financially, urged me to live with my friend and not to marry him. Do you think money has something to do with how he feels?"*

♂ *"I was lonely at first, just for a while, and my children and grandchildren came to visit, just when I was beginning to date. They drove me up the wall. My physician suggested that I tell them to leave. Now I see them in small doses and I have some energy left over for dating."*

♀ *"My children encouraged us, but his gave us a bad time. They didn't seem to think I was good enough for him. They wanted me to make up for whatever had been wrong in their parents' marriage."*

♀ "*My children tolerated one friend I had, but they didn't think he treated me right. He wouldn't go to family gatherings, so that was a problem. He made up excuses — that it would be too crowded, or that he had something else he had to do. So I went by myself. I didn't want my children to feel that I had to depend on them, at a time when all of them had left the nest. Anyway, I went on seeing that man for some time, but he never could accept the fact that I had a family of my own.*"

♂ "*I understand that in England, in the Church of England, you have to get letters from your children giving approval for a second marriage. If that were true here, mine would approve. But Mary's wouldn't; they seem to think it's too soon, even for her to be dating somone.*"

❋❋❋

WHAT DO YOU THINK OF HIM?

I had become involved with a man for the first time in years, and my son had just met him.

"What do you think of him?" I asked.

"He chews with his mouth open."

"What? What else?"

"He seems kind, nice, smart. And he has a good sense of humor. I'd be careful — go slow — however."

I was surprised. "Why? Because he chews with his mouth open?"

"No, though I remember your being fussy about that when we were growing up. I'm concerned because you haven't known him very long. And because he sounds so bitter, so angry about his divorce."

A VARIATION ON THE THEME

Gay couples usually don't have to answer to children. But this is what one partner in a long-term gay relationship told me:

"I regret, now, that I never had any children. I realized this especially when I went to a college reunion where most of the people were talking about their children and grandchildren. My special friend and I have been together for many years. He's quite a bit younger. I might have even more in common with him now if I had had children; they would be closer to his generation and then I might understand him better."

A CODA — ABOUT HARMONY

In *Indian Summer of the Heart* by Diane Newman, an elderly Quaker widower says to the woman he hopes to marry: "Most people would say that the children's wishes about their parents' relationships are irrelevant. But how can there be harmony in the world, if even parents and grown children disregard each other? We shall have to be patient. It may take time for thy children to understand."

A SAD SONG: NOTES FROM A WIDOWER'S DIARY

MONTH 1: My wife's friends are befriending me. They invite me to their homes just to meet women.

MONTH 6: I'm encouraging her friends to shake me loose. It's more fun to be on my own!

MONTH 12: Two of my friends took me aside and warned me: before you marry them, women claim they want sex, but afterwards...it's another story.

MONTH 15: I should have listened to my friends' warnings. I'd have been better off not getting married.

The only thing that's certain about the influence of friends on relationships between older men and women is that our friends have clout, and don't hesitate to use it.

One woman told me that her friends didn't think anyone would be good enough for her, because her first husband had been such a great guy. How did she handle that? She told them that she would go on seeing someone even if they didn't think he was good enough — because he might have a friend who was!

Another woman was impressed because the friends of the man she was dating were so caring and protective of him. "Also," she said, "we had mutual friends, and it was fun discovering that. We decided that we weren't going to stop seeing old friends, mutual or not."

Mutual friends can give a newly intimate couple the feeling of familiarity and trust that older people don't always have time to build. They can help to bridge the gap created by all the years of separate lives the couple had lived before they came together.

FRIENDS, INDEED

♂ *"Not one of my group of friends advised me to get married. One said: 'What will you get that you don't get now?'"*
♀ *"Some of my friends tried to be supportive. They brought me men on a platter and offered me up the same way."*
♂ *"My married friends urge me to get married and assume I can't be happy otherwise. My single friends don't."*

A FAMILIAR TUNE

Advice from friends is free, and plentiful.

♀ *"You can't count on older men. They'll never change anything about their lives for you, and they are even more demanding — you know what I mean — than younger ones. They're bigger babies, too."*
♂ *"She'll never stop talking about her first husband. And remember this: she doesn't want to hear about your first wife!"*

Fortunately, there are other kinds of friends. Like one of mine, who said:

> "He seems so nice. *There are always risks involved with love, and what better time in your life to embrace those risks?*"

V

GOING FOR IT: FOR RICHER, FOR POORER

Oh, what we seniors proclaim about the almighty dollar!

♀ *"The only man I'd marry would be 99 years old, ill, with lots of money and no family!"* *(This woman was joking, she said.)*

♂ *"I would co-habit, but probably never marry again because it would complicate my financial status."*

♀ *"I like successful men — with money. I don't want to support anyone, I don't want to scrape for money ever again."*

♂ *"I'm stuck! I give my ex-wife half of my retirement pay. There's hardly enough left for dating, or for my phone calls to another woman. They are never under $200 a month — once, I got a phone bill for $580."*

♀ *"I meet a man, I worry: could he be interested in me just to improve his own life style?"*

♂ *"Real wealth comes from within ourselves, but I'm still grappling with that. Money does take care of a lot of anxiety and fear."*

♂ *"Lack of material assets would not concern me — there are no U-hauls attached to hearses."*

WHY DON'T YOU TAKE A CRUISE?

"There were a lot of older, single women on the cruise I took last year, and only a few men like myself. That's the way most cruises are.

"One of the men I got friendly with told me he had decided some years ago that a cruise was the way to meet wealthy women, so he put all the money he could spare into one that went most of the way around the world. He did meet a woman and they became close. It wasn't until they landed back in San Francisco that he found out she had done the same thing: put all her available resources into the cruise, where she hoped to meet a rich man! In spite of that, their relationship deepened, and they married. Now this man was alone again; his wife died. He had just enough money left for this shorter cruise.

"I don't think he was looking for a wealthy widow this time. It was more a trip of nostalgia for him. He had really loved his wife, and he missed her. He didn't make much effort to meet anyone. He seemed lonely."

$ $ $

"I took a cruise once. I met an attractive woman who invited me to visit her in her California home and escort her to parties because, as she said, 'Other men are after my money, and I'm pretty sure you're not.'

"I never did find out why she thought I wasn't after her money!"

Whether you call it the root of all evil, lettuce, filthy lucre, or just cold, hard cash, money is often a crucial matter for us older people in our relationships.

Having acquired it separately during our lives, we tend to guard it zealously, especially where our children's inheritance is concerned.

♂ *"When I told my son about my plans to marry again, he said flatly, 'It's up to you.' I'm sure he was thinking about my estate, so I assured him that it would go to him and his children. The next thing I knew, he was urging me to tie the knot."*

STARS IN THEIR EYES — OR IS IT $ $?

♂ *"I was very concerned about money and having all the questions answered — who paid for what — before I proposed formally to my second wife, even though she didn't think it was romantic to talk about such things. Now I'm going with a much younger woman. She owns her own small business and is determined to get it paid off. That's part of the attraction for me."*

♂ *"On our first trip together I told her we would have to stop in a motel noted primarily for its low cost. She said, 'I wouldn't be caught dead in one.' But we stayed there a week and she didn't complain. Later, she said she could live at my level, that she wouldn't bring her wealthier past into this new situation. But it didn't work out. I'll never know how much money had to do with that; after a while she just clammed up and couldn't talk with me or relate to me at all."*

"MONEY IS OFTEN A CRUCIAL MATTER...
WE TEND TO GUARD IT ZEALOUSLY..."

♀ "*I don't tell my new husband how I feel about money. I learned in my first marriage not to bring up things that are going to cause a hassle. Besides, with my first husband we had all our life together to work things out.*"

♀ "*Money is a special problem for us. We both have our own, which we inherited, and Social Security. But we haven't worked out who spends whose money for what. Right now, my husband won't buy me a new top for my convertible and I don't want to go into my principal for it. We have a joint account but no agreement as to what it is to be used for. So far, I've only used it for food. Oh, it's all so different, so confusing compared to the way it was in my first marriage. At least, the way it was after 30 years!*"

Listen to this exchange that took place around a seniors bridge table:

Mrs. M: "I was determined to be independent. I still have my own checking account."

Mrs. R: "Me, too! I wouldn't marry a younger man who still works. I'm afraid he'd become dependent on me if he quit or got fired when I'm set for life with retirement and Social Security."

Mrs. T: "Well, I've always preferred quality. The man doesn't have to be rich, but I would want him to like nice things and to have aspired to acquiring them himself."

Mrs. B: "Hoity toity! How about this for a problem? I like to give money away, when I have it. My husband thinks I should save it. He didn't let his first wife charge anything, and he doesn't want me to. But I've always had credit cards, and I write checks. I tell people: look before you leap — look into his wallet."

These women touched on one of the subtle meanings of money. You won't find this definition in any dictionary, but here it is:

♀ *"Money means different things to different people. That's what I found and what I finally got my friend to see. He didn't realize we were really talking about* dependence and independence."

♂ *"I admire her* independence, *which she can afford. And it's driving me crazy."*

♂ *"In my last relationship the woman insisted on paying her own way. She insisted too much. Too* independent *for me!"*

♂ *"When I was young, I expected to be the sole breadwinner. Now I'm not so sure. I'm comfortable, but I would have less if I took in a mate who was* dependent *on my income. So I need someone with an income of her own. Money's not the only object, but it is one."*

♀ *"We got together because his shower went out, the temperature in his apartment was either too hot or too cold, and my place was roomier. We pooled our resources to share this apartment. Sure, each of us lost some of our* independence, *but we gained a lot more."*

♀ *"I have to be* independent. *I wouldn't want another man to share in what my husband left me."*

❋❋❋

Among all these voices, there were some who saw money as an opportunity, not a problem. As Samuel Pepys said, "It is pretty to see what money can do."

♀ *"Each of us was getting along pretty well with what we had; then we got married. Suddenly, each felt wealthy. We live well; we can even travel. But the most fun is helping our children now, while we can share in their enjoyment."*

♂ *"Sharing money is one of the special joys in relationships at this age. And it's the source for some of our best fights!"*

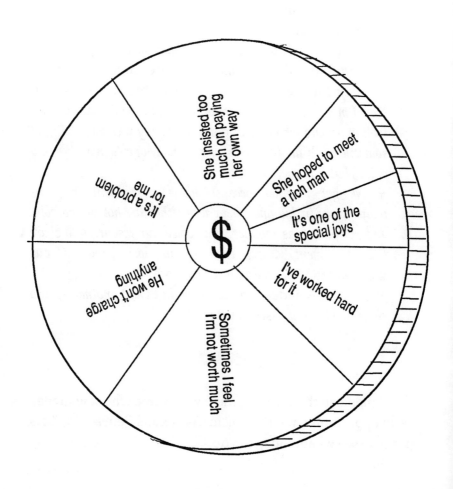

VI

GOING FOR IT: IN SICKNESS AND IN HEALTH

May 18

Dear Harry:

Ever since you left on Sunday, I've been going over all the wonderful things we talked about. You stirred up all sorts of new ideas in my head!

I'm glad we could talk about your bypass surgery. I've always believed that "in sickness and in health" would be easy to accept. Now that I'm nearly 70, I'm not so sure.

Even before my husband died, I was finding out that my friends' illnesses could rob me of their support. After David died, I didn't have anyone to confide in and I'm sure that contributed to my depression.

David and I were married 40 years. I knew he was dying so I had some preparation, but it was still very difficult. In the four years since then, I have been telling myself that I'd never want to nurse another man through an illness. Now you've made me question that. I liked what you said about not dwelling on the possibility of illness at our ages. I guess it's just that the memory of David's illness and death is still too fresh.

I'm also remembering that you said we'd be better at taking care of each other, have more compassion, because we've both already experienced the trials and tribulations of ill-health. I hope that's true, because I have a confession to make: I dreaded getting any older with David! He was a fine man, but he was also a complainer, a baby, about his ailments. I can already see that you are different, that you handle it better.

There! It was easier to write that than to tell you in person. If we're going to be together more, as we both seem to want, I'll have to try to be as open as you are in sharing what you are thinking and feeling.

I'm looking forward — so much — to seeing you again in two weeks.

My love to you,
Grace

June 1
Dear Grace:

It was a wonderful weekend! I feel that our friendship has taken a giant step forward. I wish I could be with you again this week, but I can't dodge that meeting. It's nice to be asked to participate, even when I've been inactive in the firm for five years.

At least I'm not torn in two directions, like my brother. Ed stopped by yesterday on his way back from L.A. He says that it's not easy — at 75 — to jet to Los Angeles one weekend, and San Francisco the next. He said: "When I'm dating more than one person, my body gets tired, and so does my mind!"

I'm glad you could make that "confession" to me; I have one to give you in return. For some time after Betty's death, I went out only with much younger women! That gradually changed, for a number of reasons. One was that illness became a terrible consideration, even before I knew I had a heart problem. I thought about having a stroke, for instance, and being dependent on someone who might not like the idea of taking care of me. Eventually I came to realize that you never know about illness — when and where it will strike.

I had an example in my own family. My sister had a mild heart problem and her husband had been the healthy one, always "up." She kidded him about re-marrying if she died first; it never occurred to her that she might be the survivor. But she was — her husband died of lung cancer when he was only 60.

The possibility of losing the other is ever-present, isn't it? But that can be a good thing. You and I have packed a lot of pure pleasure into our three-day weekend.

I can hardly wait for the next.

Harry.

June 7

Dear Harry:

I'll meet you at the airport at 3. You may not recognize me! I have a new hair-do and a new suit you haven't seen. It's lavender, (the suit, not my hair).

When we were together two weeks ago, you asked me if I had had any "serious" relationships since David died. I mentioned Charles. I think I should tell you more about that.

Two years ago I started seeing Charles who, like you, had had a heart attack and bypass surgery. As sometimes happens with serious illness, he saw each day as special — a gift.

But I don't think he ever took his pills without making a big production out of it. "It must be lunch time, time for my pills," he would announce, and I'd feel a twinge of annoyance every time he reached into his pocket, or his knapsack, for his pill case. Several times he showed me all the different colors, like a kid with new marbles.

When we went away together for the first time (do I shock you, Harry?) the weekend was harmonious at first. But on the last evening, after he had promised to take me to Trader Vic's as a special treat, he backed down. "I'm sorry," he said, "I can't! There just isn't enough time. It's not good for my heart to push so much. We'll have to eat in the hotel's coffee shop."

It also bothered me that he didn't do what he could to help himself. He was overweight, but couldn't stay on a diet. Once, when we had breakfast with a friend of mine, he had two helpings of waffles and bacon and sausage; later, he said he did that because he didn't want to hurt our hostess's feelings!

I was sympathetic but I had to make my own decision about whether or not I wanted to be part of his life under those circumstances. After some more experience with it, it seemed clear to me that he used his heart condition as a way of manipulating and controlling me, and as an excuse for doing what he wanted to do. Especially, to avoid dealing with conflicts. I decided I didn't want a life focused on his heart condition, so we parted.

My brother Jim, the one who's a doctor, wasn't a bit sympathetic. He said that my attitude might come from a lack of medical knowledge, that my friend probably had angina, which is excruciatingly painful. Jim said: "If he didn't let it interfere with your walks, or whatever, I think that shows a lot of strength on his part." But that wasn't the way I felt about it.

I may have been influenced by my mother, too. Her contemporaries had a saying: "Are you going to be a nurse, or a purse?" And one time when my father was ill, she kept saying he was acting like a little boy. Once, when they were having an argument about something else, I heard my father yelling that she didn't understand how crucial it was to him to maintain peace of mind, not to talk about their problems — because of his heart condition.

Now you know, Harry, where I'm coming from when it comes to that subject! We can talk about that some more — and about a lot of other things — next weekend.

Impatiently,

Grace

..."HE WAS ACTING LIKE A LITTLE BOY."

June 15

Dear Grace:

First, I want to thank you for another wonderful weekend! I hope I convinced you of what I have become convinced: that you and I have a future together. When you come up here next month, and we're together for a longer time, and you meet the rest of my family, I hope any lingering questions you might have will be answered.

I have suddenly learned, first hand (that's a pun!) that when you are old, and alone, you shouldn't break any bones! Now don't worry — it's only my wrist. I fell clumsily on a slippery brick path, and now I'm sporting a cast on my arm. The worst of it is that I can't even button my pants. "Wish you were here" takes on a new meaning!

I enjoyed meeting your daughters. What did they have to say about us — about me?

Dearest Grace, I must apologize for what I said about the possibility of ours being a very short relationship. I hope you really did understand what I meant. It really isn't a *negative* or *pessimistic* thing. It's just a fact. Any woman your age would have to know that a relationship with a man three years older could be a very short one! I think of that as contributing to the intensity — to the delights — of whatever time we do have together.

I have plans for convincing you of this when you come up here. Wear your new suit again and I'll tell you what *that* does to my aging heart!

All my love,

Harry

June 22

Dear Harry:

This will be my last letter to you before I board that plane for my trip north to your home. My thoughts are racing ahead.

You asked about my daughters and their reaction to you. Both like you a lot, but then I hadn't worried about that. Jenny — always the cynic — worries because I didn't use the word "marriage." She said something like, "He'll marry you when he needs someone to take care of him." She also said she thinks it may be hard for you to let people take care of you. Is that true?

Beth said that one of the questions she and her sorority sisters used to ask themselves about prospective pledges was, "Would you want to brush your teeth next to this girl?" She asked me to adapt that to my situation and ask myself if I would want to take care of you if you became seriously ill. I know the answer to that one now! I'll tell you next week, in person.

All my love,

Your

Grace

✱✱✱

Harry and Grace faced questions about their health and resolved them; they married and lived happily ever after — however long that was.

Men and women over 60 handle their health problems in different ways, especially when they think about those problems in relation to each other.

♂ *"If I'm sick I don't give in to it. I haven't taken any medicine or seen a doctor in 17 years.* I go into a secret place in my mind and work it out. *I might not be as patient with another person if they gave in to it easily."*

♀ *"I don't want to be a burden. I'm too old.* I'll stay alone."

♂ *"At my age, you can't operate if you don't accept the prospect of death. But if I were a burden to a woman, and aware of it,* I would disappear."

♀ *"My husband is 80 and he's in a convalescent home. I'm 82. He still depends on me. I had emphysema, and* gave up smoking *because I knew I had to outlive him."*

♂ *"My solution to having a heart problem is this:* I have a right to be selfish, *even if it hurts people around me. My life may depend on it."*

♀ *"Even more than when I first asked myself, I know now that* I would wait on him hand and foot if he needed that. *I love him."*

♂ *"Let the woman take care of her man, if she wants to! For some, that's their self-image. It works out o.k. if the man wants to be taken care of."*

♂ *"I had a close friend who had TB and his wife, considerably younger, refused to stay and take care of him.* She just walked out."

♀ *"I know women who won't get involved with older men because of their concerns about their health. The big risk is the feeling of being abandoned by one or the other, by death if not in other ways.* Both people have to be willing to risk!"

VII

GOING FOR IT: TILL DEATH DO US PART
SIDNEY AND MIRIAM

The voice on the telephone was matter-of-fact. "My name is Miriam S. I heard that you are interviewing older couples who have married recently. Would you like to talk to my husband and me?"

The first hint that this was an unusual story came when we were arranging to meet. "Can you come to the hospice?" Miriam asked. Striving to match her calmness, I said, "Sure."

On first glance, it was obvious that Sidney was very ill. His skin was shriveled and yellow. He was lying in bed, apparently asleep, and he stirred only when Miriam touched him gently and told him I was there. Slowly, he held out a very thin, bony hand. I took it; his hand felt like a piece of crumpled parchment.

As we talked, he moved restlessly in bed, often scratching his arms with a brush he kept on the bedside table. "The itching is awful," he said with a small smile.

Sidney and Miriam had known each other seven years. They met when Miriam and her first husband came from their home in the east to go on a cruise up the west coast. Sidney was on the ship too, a widower, alone again after a good marriage of 44 years. They became a threesome. After the trip, Sidney corresponded with Miriam and her husband over the years. Then Miriam's husband died. Sidney called her to commiserate, and although they hadn't talked for seven years, once having begun they kept calling, talking, and writing.

"After two years of this, we knew each other better than a lot of people who have been married," Miriam said, handing me a cup of tea brought in by the attentive hospice nurse.

In one of his early letters, Sidney told Miriam that he would never consider marrying again. "I liked my freedom," Sidney told me now. "I could take a trip, go to school, do whatever I wanted.

"I didn't want to surrender that franchise. But the thing with Miriam just grew. I'm glad it was that way before I knew I was ill."

Miriam found special joy in being close to someone again. "That was a surprise," she said. "I didn't know I wanted that again." Sidney said to me: "You asked us, as everyone has, why we married. That answers the question for both of us."

Sidney continued. "We had planned that I would come to Florida, where Miriam was living, in April. And if we were as compatible as we thought we would be, we would marry and I'd move there, where she had a larger home. We had reservations for a cruise to South America in September, and more travel planned. Both of us had kept the growing relationship to ourselves; we hadn't even told our families. We thought we would lose control of the situation if we told people about it and it didn't work out."

Sidney had brushed aside concerns about his health while these plans were being made. He often felt exhausted, and there were unexplained pains. Then one day he went to a Jacuzzi and "my power went off," he said. He fainted, and was taken to a local hospital, where tests provided a distressing diagnosis: cancer of the pancreas, too far advanced for treatment.

"I called Miriam and told her about it," Sidney related calmly. "She said she would take the first plane out."

"Then I told my family and friends about Sidney," Miriam interjected. "They were shocked. 'What does he look like?' someone asked. I had to say I didn't know, exactly; I hadn't seen him for seven years."

All the way out on the plane, Miriam wondered about what she was doing. After her first husband died, she had thought she could never marry again, as theirs had been a very good marriage, a very close relationship. With Sidney she foresaw other problems, as well: she was used to a 12-room house in Florida, he to a studio apartment in California. They both had families.

"When I came out to California, I planned to stay and take care of Sidney," Miriam continued. "I had only packed one suitcase; I had no idea how long I would be staying."

"We were married in March," Sidney said, with a grin that stretched the thin skin of his jaundiced face.

Inevitably, I asked again why they married, when they knew Sidney would live only a few months, at best. They had mentioned the joys of closeness; was that really enough?

"It was like a jigsaw puzzle," Sidney explained, as though it were that simple. "Each piece only fits in one place. Or it's like a key for a lock. We felt that we were building on a firm foundation." Other people asked why they could not be satisfied with the relationship they had. "Because this is a permanent relationship, not a transient one," Sidney had told them. "Each of us needs the other. It's vital. And that's what marriage is."

For a wedding present, Sidney's nephew took them to dinner at a very special restaurant. Miriam laughed. "That's the only time when we've ever been out together in the evening!"

They had a church wedding. She wore a blue dress she had brought with her. Sidney's pals at the retirement complex were happy for them, and supportive; they called Sidney and Miriam "the kids."

It was not only a busy time, it was "worrisome and frustrating," according to Sidney. "But the fact that we were together made it a project." Miriam: "He isn't an A-1 housekeeper." Sidney: "She is an A-plus plus." Miriam: "He had 10 years' accumulation but was good about getting rid of things."

Miriam thought that in a month's time she could take Sidney back to Florida with her, but his physician said, "No traveling." So they stayed. One of their many problems was that Sidney's daughter and granddaughter, who lived close by, didn't see the necessity of their getting married. "We had to combat that and still keep a good relationship with them," Miriam said. "It turned out as well as it could under the circumstances."

But although Sidney's daughter came to accept their marriage, Miriam still does not feel entirely comfortable with her. "She is very aggressive; I'm a passive person. I have to be very careful." Miriam realizes that the younger woman didn't know her at all and may have wondered if she was a "golddigger." Then too, Miriam was 12 years younger than Sidney and only 10 years older than his daughter.

The couple had a good life together for several weeks. Sidney, an investment counselor all his life, directed Miriam's research into financial planning, which she found fascinating. They also began to see what their problems would have been, if they could have counted on more time together.

"I can't imagine two people with less in common," Miriam said. Sidney responded with a smile. "The only reason it worked was all that time we spent writing to each other, especially the last four months before Miriam came out here. We didn't have to go through a period of getting to know each other."

Some of their differences were about standards — their own and those where they lived. "We might have had a problem if I had gone to Florida," Sidney said, "there's quite a rigid dress code there." Miriam said that her life style was completely different from his. "But I think we would have worked it out. I would have sold my home so we could look at condominiums as a base for all the traveling we wanted to do."

The difference in their ages was important only because of his illness, they believe. "He fought my taking it on," Miriam said. "But I was very willing and would do it again. I chose to."

They might have had a problem about grooming, Sidney ventured. "She can spot a spot 30 yards away. I'm artistic, but I can't see what I am doing when I am putting outfits together." (This is in part because he had lost most of the sight in one eye.) "So I decided to put things together for him," Miriam said. "Usually, it was o.k., but sometimes he would balk and I would back off. I don't like dissension."

"She's much more conventional," Sidney said, reaching for Miriam's hand. "I've always been a freewheeler; I always considered myself a loner. I had to make some adjustments."

Miriam spoke of her brothers, older enough to be of a different generation. "I was the little kid that didn't know anything." She took care of her mother for years. Now she is taking care of Sidney. But also: "I can't let him sleep all the time — I need him!"

Their life together broadened until Sidney started going downhill physically. On Easter Sunday, he collapsed. His physician didn't think Miriam could continue to take care of him in his apartment, so they went to the hospice. Sidney: "We knew that day was coming, but it came much too fast."

*** ✱✱✱ ***

Five days after I met Sidney and Miriam, Sidney died. A week later, I received a letter from Miriam. She said that Sidney had hoped to dictate a final letter to his friends, but he completed only one paragraph before weakness claimed him. Here it is:

"Yo-ho-ho and a bottle of rum. Land dead ahead.
It has been a long voyage lasting over 70 years.
I have been through storms and sailed through sunshine.
I have been whipped across huge seas and
    been lulled in the breeze of the major oceans.
I have been frantic in the fog, but fearless
    on the open sea."

Miriam's letter to me continued: "And thus — the passing of a most interesting person — highly intelligent, dynamic, curious, an independent thinker, determined, fearless, a great conversationalist, people oriented and above all else, honest. He will be missed in so many ways by so many people."

And then she concluded: "I plan to continue living here in our apartment until the end of June or longer, if it seems necessary. I shall then return to Florida."

VIII

"WE THOUGHT YOU'D NEVER ASK!"

What do seniors say about sex?
No thanks...
Yes, but...
Where do I sign up?

NO THANKS

The "no thanks" group has its own factions: those who just don't want to bother any more; those who had it so good that they don't want to threaten their memories with any new, less satisfying experiences; those who because of "engine failure" can't — or think they can't.

In her autobiography, Enid Bagnold refers to "the pain of sex, the love like a wild fox so ready to bite, the antagonism that sits like a twin beside love."

It is that aspect of sex which turns off many older people, especially those of us who yearn for another kind of love described by Bagnold: "the affection, so deeply unrepeatable, of two people who have lived a life together." Denied that affection, we won't risk sex. Some of us fall back on masturbation, the satisfaction we discovered as adolescents. Others simply do without.

> ♂ *"It's too much work. Women my age still want to be 'wooed,' to be brought along gradually. Who's got time for that when they're 70?"*
>
> ♀ *"I had my first date about six months after my husband died. The man took me to dinner where there was music, and candlelight. 'Do you think you could enjoy sexual intercourse to relieve tension without getting involved emotionally?' he asked. I said I guessed not."*
>
> ♀ *"I'm not a person who masturbates. I'm a Baptist."*

With hindsight, many imperfect marriages take on an aura of perfection. The survivor of one of these "made-in-heaven" marriages may be protective of his or her memories, choosing not to disturb or challenge them with new, chancy experiences.

> ♀ *"I can't imagine sharing a bed with a man again. My husband and I were married 30 years before he died; I'd feel that I was being unfaithful to him."*

One woman was upset when her doctor asked her if she was active sexually.

"Of course not!" she told him. "I wouldn't want to mar my experience with my husband by having a bad sexual experience now. I wouldn't feel proud of myself. My husband's spirit is with me."

Men have their own concerns, including impotency or the threat of impotency. Others who still crave sex think of themselves as abnormal, while some plunge right in. It is their way of keeping the fear of impotency at bay.

♂ *"Good sex tells me that I'm still o.k., at a time when I'm letting go of my career, my grown children, some of my friends — who are dying."*

♂ *"I've had 16 affairs since my divorce two years ago. I get lots of overtures from women my own age, but I don't relate to them other than for companionship. I like younger women because of my sexual inclinations and sex drive."*

However, that 60-year-old man candidly admitted that he hadn't had any sexual experience with older women.

✳✳✳

In the play "Sand Dollar Cove" by Keith McGregor, Jason (67) and Pat (73), newly acquainted, are sharing their thoughts and feelings about many things for the first time.

JASON:....just when we were startin' to take it easy, enjoy life, do some travellin', she had to up and die.

PAT: How old was she?

JASON: Sixty-four.

PAT: Awful young. My Stephen was only fifty-one, but he was in a car wreck. A widow at forty-six, and I'd been married nearly thirty years.

JASON: Almost forty for us. I still can't get used to her being gone. You wake up in the morning and she ought'a be there.

PAT: That'll pass.

JASON: I'm not sure I want it to.

PAT: Oh the memories'll stay; but the pain'll pass. Not totally. I don't think it should; unless maybe you meet someone else.

JASON: She told me I ought'a get married again.

PAT: If you meet the right person, why not? But only if you want to be with that person; not so you'll forget Susan. I never met anyone I could live with.

JASON: I probably won't either.

PAT: You might. Just don't rush it. Love isn't like a hole that's there and you can just go find it an' jump right in.

JASON: I'm not talking about love. Just somebody to do things with; take trips; somebody to talk to.

PAT: You've completely written off sex?

JASON: (an embarrassed chuckle): I don't know. Maybe not.

PAT: Don't. It's better'n walking for keeping you young.

JASON: At my age, there's definitely more exercise in walking.

PAT: I don't mean exercise; I mean attitude. Being able to..."do it" is great for your self-esteem. I've read all about it. Personally speaking, I wouldn't know about such things. Besides, you're not an old man yet.

JASON: I sure as hell feel like it.

❋❋❋

When a man has been impotent for a number of years, this is often a significant factor in his attitude about marriage, or even about relationships. That's especially true when a potential partner is operating under the banner of "no sex without marriage and no marriage without sex."

Sometimes it's society that assumes aging and sex don't go together. Or one's children. Even professionals, who should know better. One gynecologist asked his 62-year-old patient why she was getting married again: "Just for companionship?"

Her spirited reply: "No! Who needs companionship? I need sex!"

During one 70-year-old woman's annual physical exam, her physician didn't think to ask about her sexual activity. She had to bring it up herself.

"Do you have any advice for me about...you know, the physical side of things?"

Startled, he blurted out: "Let nature take its course!"

YES, BUT...

- There isn't enough time to work it out, to make adjustments.
- She said she'd been to bed with 65 men. I wasn't going to be number 66.
- Sex is a poor excuse for taking on housework.
- I would have to be able to use the word "love," and mean it.
- I'm G.I. — geographically impossible.
- I'm still a one-woman man.
- I wear dentures. Should I tell him that, or let him find out for himself when he kisses me?

•Men don't give you a chance to get to know them first.
•Now that I'm 80, sex has to be different. Friendlier.
•I get goosepimples just dancing with a man — I'm afraid of being touched.
•I've a greater void to fill, first. I want to find answers to some other questions about myself.

"I say my sap's still running strong
  I'm even rather flirty
  (My son) says what's great at 35
  At 66 is dirty."

Grandpa's Playpen Blues by Irene Paull

WHERE DO I SIGN UP?

The possibility that sex can be better with age is a tempting thought. Physical limitations may negate this for some, but for others — yes, the best is yet to be.

♀ *"He had a reservoir of urge built up, and I did, too."*
♂ *"What drew us together? Sex! Sex as I never knew it could exist. We just have a plain good old time together."*
♀ *"One man suggested that we take a shower together. My husband and I had never done that; it struck me as quite risque, and fun. Yet I hesitated. I had a pretty good idea of what his body looked like and, loving him, accepted it. But that didn't stop me from worrying about how I would look to him — naked in the harsh light of the bathroom. Could he accept my 65-year-old body? I decided what the hell. It was great fun!"*

"MY HUSBAND AND I HAD NEVER DONE THAT. "

My friend who runs a small wedding chapel observes: "One woman in her seventies told me that her appreciation for her fiance's caring had a lot to do with her happiness. It was something she had been finding it harder and harder to come by.

"As for sex — with the very young, it's still a novelty. Older couples know what they want, have put more thought into it."

Psychiatrist Mai-Britt Rosenbaum, speaking on TV, said that midlife can be a wonderfully expanding time for a woman. She has the experience of how it feels to be sexual. She is more comfortable with her sexuality, and therefore more willing to take risks.

"Her parents' warning voices have faded," Dr. Rosenbaum said. "The body has become known to her, less of a mystery. Also, the sense of time left adds poignancy to the here and now. She has more self-confidence and balance in her relationships as men change, too, and become more aware of their tender, receiving aspects."

Indeed, the times are "a-changin'." Today, the admonition for older people to "act their age" can mean that they use all their experience in the service of their later years.

> ♂ "We were having a lovely time in bed — our first time — when her daughter came home early from a date, and came in to say goodnight to her mother. What saved the evening was that we were grown up — we could laugh about it."
> ♀ "I had no idea it could be like this; it was as though we lost all our inhibitions with age!"

✳✳✳

They perch on the edge of a couch in their motel room — a couple in their eighties who had been married the day before. Both have white hair; hers is tightly curled, his sparse. He is portly, she is slim and bird-like, fluttery.

"He came up and asked me if I would like to dance," she says. "I love to dance! That's how it began."

They had known each other casually for years; her second husband had worked with him. They met again — both now alone — at a company dinner for retirees.

"He sent me an orchid for our first date," his bride recalls. He explains: "We were going to dinner Saturday night. I ordered the orchid Friday, so I would be committed to showing up."

Their compatibility was immediate. "If we had met when were younger, we might have gotten married and still would be," he says.

"I'd been alone for more than four years," she explains. "I was very particular, especially about people I was meeting for the first time."

"But our friends, and our children, encouraged us. And now I had an escort. He was wonderful — gifts every time."

"That made me feel good," he says. "Neither of us had had an unhappy marriage, but we did have the circumstances of having tragedy and illness behind us. That led to our having compassion for each other. And we were too old to wait! Even so, our mutual friends wondered why we waited so long to get married — six months!"

After an hour or so, I close my notebook, hug them both and leave them standing in the doorway with their arms around each other. It isn't until the next day that I realize I didn't ask them about one important facet of their marriage. I had been too shy. I phone them and tentatively put forth the question.

"We thought you'd never ask!" they chorus. "Our sex life is great!"

IX

FRANCES: "BUT WHAT IS TIME?"

I first met Frances backstage. Our senior center was producing its annual play and I was the "prop" person. Frances sewed and patched and altered our well-worn costumes. We spent many hours together backstage during rehearsals, or seated in the small theater as we watched the play unfold.

I liked watching Frances work. At 71, she is tall and slim, with lightly waved white hair full and soft around her face. There are only a few fine lines around her eyes and mouth. Even with her cane, Frances moves gracefully.

This is her story.

FRANCES

I like working on these costumes; it reminds me of the years when I made costumes for my daughters — for school plays and Girl Scouts. Those were very happy years and they continued right up until my husband died suddenly, after a heart attack.

I didn't want to marry again. Within six months I knew that I could make a life for myself, alone. I had had an art gallery, and I went back to it. My social life evolved around couples and other women. I would have welcomed the idea of a platonic relationship with a man but I never met anyone for that.

Then a friend invited me to a party — dinner for eight. At first I said I was just too tired. I was reluctant, because I'd been to lots of these dinners and I always felt like a fifth wheel. But my friend insisted, saying that she needed me to even out the group. I told myself, "Well, all right — just one more."

My first impression of Robert that night was that he was desperate. It was obvious that he didn't know what he was going to do now that his wife had died and he had retired from the military. He seemed to be a man who had been taken care of by others all his life; he had always had junior officers to serve him, as well as his wife. I felt sorry for him, and that was it.

Then I remembered reading a helpful article about surviving the loss of a spouse, and I sent it to him. He was grateful, and phoned to tell me so. We talked a long time and then he asked me out to dinner.

We had a lovely evening together. Watching him, I wondered why I had not seen, the first time, how attractive he was. By the time we said goodnight, I was glowing. It was marvelous! A romance with a wonderful man.

He called me early the morning after our dinner date, and invited me to see his apartment. That week we went to a concert and one beautiful evening we had supper on the beach. Within a very short time I realized that I had never felt that way about anyone, not even my first husband.

Six weeks after we met, Robert invited me to go up to the wine country for a few days. I worried about that...I hoped he wouldn't get bored with me. And I didn't know what sort of arrangements he would make for the inn up there. I didn't even know what to wear! I spent hours shopping, and nothing I saw seemed just right. Then I realized I had a dress in my closet that would be fine, and slacks...

The weekend was wonderful. All the things I worried about.... He had arranged for separate rooms at the inn and I was relieved, but... well, I was disappointed, too. I had bought a new nightgown, just in case.

Robert was very loving that weekend. When he brought me home, he said, "On our next trip together, one key for both of us!"

I did get another chance to model my new nightgown for him.

Then, Robert proposed. It should have been the happiest day of my life. I couldn't wait to tell my daughters. The oldest sensed some hesitation; I dismissed that by saying I just wasn't sure that I could be the wife for Robert that I wanted to be. But there was something more...a premonition that flickered across my mind even as I spoke. The shadow passed as quickly as it had come.

Most of my friends were delighted by the news that Robert and I were going to be married. For a few, delight may have been tempered by envy. Wives of some of Robert's friends had had someone else in mind for him, so they were unhappy about it. One woman was quite upset because I wasn't in their circle of friends!

We were married quietly on the terrace of a friend's home in northern California, in the wine country. It was a beautiful day in every way; our families and a few close friends celebrated with us. Robert was involved in a consulting job, so we delayed our honeymoon and it was nearly a year before we started out on a trip to Europe. I remember that when I closed the door on our home, I had some reluctance to leave that happy place. But the first two weeks, which we spent in England and France, were more than a honeymoon. They was an intense coming together, a deeper sharing. I'll never forget those two weeks.

Then, in Italy, the nightmare. It began about two o'clock in the morning. We were in a hotel at the edge of a beautiful lake.

I awoke to the sound of glass breaking. Then talking, yelling — it seemed to come from some distance. Robert stirred and I turned to him immediately. Simultaneously, we were both aware of smoke that was rapidly filling our room, great gray clouds of it. We got up, ran to the window and found ourselves in a strange, frightening world: everything was obscured by the smoke. We were calm at first; I let Robert take charge.

I wanted to rush out the door. But Robert put his hand on it, said it wouldn't be safe; the fire was in the hall as well as above and below us. That was the most awful moment of my life, or so I thought. I didn't know that the worst was yet to come.

It seemed as if the only option was staying there and burning to death. We didn't hear any sirens, there was nothing to tell us that help was on the way. When the first flames shot out from the bathroom area, Robert said, "You have to jump." We were on the second floor, but I couldn't see the ground from the window because of the smoke. "Jump?" I said stupidly. "But I can't. It's too far."

Robert said it was the only thing to do. He took me by the hand and half-led, half-pushed me to the window. He kissed me and said he would follow.

I have no recollection of how I got myself out the window, or of jumping. I hope it never comes back to me, although the psychiatrist at the Navy hospital said that it might, eventually. The last thing I remember was Robert's hurried kiss. The next thing was waking up in the hospital with a cast on my leg, a very sore throat, and the most awful back pain. It was several days before I learned that my fall had been broken by an awning at the first floor. I went through it.

I asked about Robert; no one would tell me, until my oldest daughter came. By then, I knew, anyway. My daughter said that a reporter she talked to after the fire told her he thought he had seen Robert trying to help a woman who was letting herself down from the room above ours, but he couldn't be sure.

I knew; it was so like Robert to do that. In those first few days I wished, so many times, that he had not been so unselfish, so giving. But then he wouldn't have been Robert, would he?

I feel that my life stopped that night in the hotel. I will not consider marriage again. I have the same approach I had before I met Robert: I would enjoy a platonic friendship so I could do the things I did when I had an escort. But I really don't care to know any single men. My life no longer lies in that direction.

I believe each of us is here for a reason, however, and I just have to find out what that reason is. One of the things that has become even more important to me now is a chance to help younger people. Robert and I had already agreed to help some of our younger relatives who need loans for college expenses. I'm doing that, and more. Robert's grandson is a fine young musician; he needs help if he is going to go to the best schools.

I know I've still got a lot to work through; I'm not as together as I seem on the surface. But I'll make it. I don't know if there is life after death; I want to think so, but I don't, not really. So I don't know if Robert will ever know about the rest of my life, without him. But I'll know, and I like to think that I'm a better, stronger person because of him, because of our love. So I'll just have to live that way, won't I?

I'm not sorry — not at all — that I met and married Robert. Only that we had so little time together. But what is time? We made the most of what we had.

X

YOUR PLACE — OR MINE?

GARAGE SALE! Two families become one. Fabrics, books, china, furniture, even the kitchen sink! Saturday, 9 a.m. Sunset Drive

---

Two homes. The owner of one is a collector and a teacher of interior design. She has 14 boxes of fabrics in her garage and every inch of the house is filled with "things that matter." The second house is larger. The owner, a sports journalist, has filled all available space with books about sports, and memorabilia. This garage sale is the first step in establishing one home, together.

Compromise is the name of the game. This couple has decided to live in the larger house and rotate their possessions. She said: "For a couple of months I'll have my special things out, and then I'll store those and he'll put out some of his."

While acknowledging that possessions are not as important as being comfortable in his house, the bride-to-be cried over some teacups that were gifts for her first wedding, 30 years before. She had planned to take them to an auction studio, but couldn't do it. They would find room.

He was surprised to see that he had three boxes of cornstarch in his cupboard and four bottles of syrup. He also found he had a special feeling for certain knives and bowls; he secretly hoped that no one would buy them.

Such attachments to objects are common. One man was especially fond of a chaise longue that had belonged to his first wife. His second wife tried to convince herself that she loved it too, but she didn't.

"It was covered in a big bold print, not my kind of thing at all. Finally I realized that it wasn't just the chaise I objected to, it was my husband's attachment to his first wife. We managed to talk about it, and before long, the chaise disappeared. By then it would have been o.k. with me if it had stayed!"

HOME FOR SALE. Two bedrooms, one bath. Priced for quick sale; owner moving to larger home.

♀ *"I'd consider living with someone, sharing a house, if there are two bathrooms and we each took care of our own. I'm not about to pick up after someone else now."*

♀ *"The home we settle in should be large enough to afford each of us some privacy. That's especially important when you are older."*

IT WASN'T JUST THE CHAISE I OBJECTED TO.

♂ *"She made me feel at home here, not as a guest, but as a husband. So we are living here and use my apartment when we go to the city for the theater, concerts."*

OLDER HOME FOR SALE. With some remodeling could be a showcase. Great for handyman or interior decorator.

♂ *"I'm a little pissed off because I'm spending three months fixing up this house for her, the way she wants it, and I don't have time for anything else."*

♂ *"We've been living in my house since we got married last year. Our home had been furnished by another woman, of course — my first wife. I said let's live with it for a while. Only recently have I come around to letting my new wife change things. We have different tastes, but they aren't so far apart. We're still working on making it ours. We haven't had any arguments — just a not-settled feeling."*

♀ *"I'm happy to know that I get to stay here indefinitely. In my first marriage we had to move frequently because of company transfers. I'll bide my time about making changes; I'll slip in a little change here and there."*

♀ *"We live in his house and I love it. But it was hard at first. He didn't want me to hang a picture or change anything. The situation was complicated by the fact that his daughter was living with us for a while; she liked things the way they were, too. I decided to take the bull by the horns, so to speak; I just plowed in and spent some of my own money to redecorate the house. Then he started bragging about it to his friends. It's becoming our home."*

> **BRAND NEW HOME FOR SALE.**
> **Spacious, convenient , perfect for newlyweds.**

♂ *"I don't think I could move into a woman's house, at least not one she had shared with another man. I'd want one that had not been either hers, or mine. It would be living with too many memories."*

♂ *"My house is for sale. My kids are pretty unhappy about it, because it's where they grew up and they still love to come back to it. But I want to make that move. It's too big, to begin with. But the main thing is that it's so thoroughly identified with my wife, with our marriage. I may never marry again, but even when women are guests in my home now, I can feel my wife's presence, the weight of all the years we spent here together. It's not fair to my guests, or to me."*

> **HOME AND HAPPINESS FOR SALE. What could be more important, whether it's a starter home or a retirement paradise? See Horizon Homes.**

♀ *"I think now that I should have realized right from the start that there would be problems with one man I was interested in. I was so excited about showing him my small apartment for the first time, and I was deflated immediately by his reaction. 'It's so small,' he said. 'You can't be comfortable here. You need a home and a garden..' I looked around at the rooms that meant so much to me — refuge, haven, delight, convenience. It was all I needed for the new life I was building for myself. But because it was early in our relationship I didn't say anything. Then when I was in his home, I was appalled by the confusion and disorder, and said so. He laughed. I let myself feel amused, at first.*

"But later, when he urged me to move in with him, I couldn't. I knew that he would probably never change, never be a tidy person. That was o.k. for him, but not for me; not at this time of my life. And I guess I was also carrying along that impression from the first time he saw my apartment...that he was the kind of man who only sees things through his own eyes..."

♂ "One reason we aren't living together or getting married is that neither of us is willing to move."

♀ "My first husband built the house I'm living in now. Even so, I can hardly wait to have a man come and share it with me."

♂ "I'll be damned if I'll move into a woman's house!"

♀ "All this business about homes can be pretty seductive. One big reason I married my second husband was that he cared so much about the home I was setting up after my divorce. I had been associating mostly with women; it was very nice being with him — his mind, his energy, his helping in my home. He painted my whole kitchen for me and put roses on the table when he finished. When we got married, he gave up many of his own possessions to move in with me. I loved him for that."

♀ "His first marriage was a happy one, but I can understand his wanting to make a fresh start in a new home. I have been divorced twice; both times I couldn't wait to move into something of my own."

♂ "I love my home in the country, even though I realize that by staying there I have cut down on my chances to meet women. I don't think I'll marry again, because I wouldn't want to give up this house."

♂ "When we were first married, my wife wanted to go on living in her own home and that's what we did for a couple of years. But something kept nagging at us to move and when we saw this house, we did. Our marriage has taken on new life."

> Evelyn Hanson
> And
> Howard Dailey
> Request The Honor Of Your Presence
> At Their Wedding
> in the meadow, at Pilot's Point
> August 27, 1988
> 4:00 p.m.
> Reception: Horizon Homes
> Garage Sale to follow

XI

"WHAT'S PAST IS PROLOGUE"

The Tempest by William Shakespeare

Do earlier marriages have a significant influence on later relationships and marriage? "Yes!" chorus older men and women. But whether that influence is for better or for worse is another matter.

Indeed, "there is something beyond the grave..." Imagine these exchanges between widowers and their dear departed wives.

"I put you on a pedestal"
"Yes, dear. That may make it hard for you to look at anyone else realistically now!"

"I don't want to marry again. I spent many years learning to love you; I don't want to start off again with anyone else."
"Oh, too bad. That doesn't say much for our marriage!"

"THERE IS SOMETHING BEYOND THE GRAVE..."

"How will any other woman and I get our two worlds together? All that conditioning each of us has to our first spouses, our children."

"Just keep trying! You have to think that your new relationship has nothing to do with ours, and get used to a new personality. Sure, it will be difficult, after you grew up and had babies with me. Be glad you have more time to spend on it than you had when we started off."

"I have you to thank for my present happiness, dear. If each of us in my new marriage had not been happily married before, had not worked through a lot of things, we never would have made it this time."

"You're welcome!"

"You'll have to admit our married life — yours and mine — was pretty rough. I'm determined to do it better this time."

"Good luck! You'll need it!"

"From up there where you are, did you see what happened at my second wedding? I broke down and cried. My new wife took my hand and held it. The preacher said, 'Well, it's happened before.' Do you know why I was crying?"

"Let me guess...you were crying for me? Well, if you can't cry for your wife of 50 years, who can you cry for?"

Even if one is divorced, rather than widowed, the influence of a first marriage is significant. Some older men and women are afraid of repeating a bad marriage; others are anxious to replace a bad experience with a good one. Many, like this man, go through various stages of adjustment and personal growth:

"My divorce was the first in our Catholic family. I had tried to salvage the marriage; I was afraid of losing my family, everything. After the divorce I came to feel there had to be something more than my everyday existence. I started on a personal quest.

"It hasn't been easy. I was so angry about the divorce that I contemplated murder, not suicide! When I was dating, right after that, I had adolescent feelings of rejection every time I got turned down. It took me a while to get over all that. I married again, briefly; that didn't work out. My life was still not together.

"Since then I have deliberately not been involved with anyone, not even in friendship. My crystal ball has been smashed so many times. I am working now to eliminate resentment and anger from my consciousness. Maybe then I'll be ready for a relationship."

Other reactions after divorce or separations:

♀ *"My two divorces were the most distasteful things in my life. But this is the first time I have ever been alone for long and I'm miserable."*

♂ *"I married again to get everything I didn't have the first time."*

♂ *"My gay relationship is the better because I had a long relationship with a woman some years ago. I first learned intimacy from her."*

♀ *"My husband and I were divorced nearly a year ago, after a long marriage. I'm just beginning to feel whole again. It takes so long finding my way. My husband was a nervous person, negative. Now I want the opposite — someone who is kind and sweet and calm. But I don't know how it would be to adapt to someone else's way of living."*

♀ *"My first husband was an alcoholic. He recovered, but the marriage had died long before. Now...well, it's totally different...comfortable. We have fun! And I can be myself. My first marriage refined what I want now — an emphasis on trust."*

BRING IN THE CLONES?

♀ *"After my husband died, I wanted to get involved immediately if I could find the right person. I thought I would meet someone as comfortable and pleasant as he. But it wasn't that easy. You have to start over. I was so accustomed to having men in my life — father, husband, three sons. But then I had to learn to live alone, to take responsibility for my home and for my husband's business. I realized I'd been sheltered! Also, I continued to think of myself as a one-man woman; I didn't give up...I stayed selective. I'm still very careful. I'm still single."*

♀ *"I know I can't replace my first husband. We did everything together; we were best friends. Maybe you only get one of those in a lifetime."*

♂ *"I'm interested in comparisons. I do try to see in what ways someone is like or different from my wife. And then what is attractive about the similarities and the differences."*

♀ *"Some men think all women are alike; if they have been rejected, they see rejection everywhere. I was seeing a divorced man who was still bitter about his divorce, which he had not wanted. When I told him that my son and his wife were separating he said, 'Oh, she kicked him out, did she?' Which was not the case. That attitude caused all kinds of problems for us."*

♀ *"If I marry again, I'd rather marry a divorced man than a widower because when someone dies you always think better of them than they were; and you compare."*

TIME AND TIDE

Whether a new relationship works well or not often depends on how well each of us is able to let go of a former relationship. Timing is all-important.

♂ *"My second marriage had a rocky start. She was divorced after less than four years in her marriage and had remained single for the next 30 years, while I had a long marriage followed by less than one year as a widower. We worked hard to bridge that difference in our experiences and I think our marriage is all the stronger for it."*

♀ *"My new husband insisted on waiting a full year after his wife's death before getting married again, while he thought it was o.k. for me to marry after only six months."*

♂ *"Our relationship held great promise, but it didn't work out. I think it was because we were in such different places in relation to our earlier marriages. She was where I had been five years before, still working through her separation and divorce. There was so little time, and yet...she wasn't ready."*

MULTIPLICATION TABLES

Multiple prior marriages (or relationships) color the future in complex ways. Each kaleidoscope is unique!

♂ *"I worked through two marriages and 18 affairs of at least three months each. At one time I was interested in marriage. Now it's day-to-day enjoyment. I'm free. Some of my women friends who have their own homes have wanted me to live there with them, but that wouldn't work. I'm spoiled by a seven-year relationship where a woman came to live with me in my house."*

♀ *"I'm 80 and I've been married just two months. My new wedding ring brings together all the stages of my life...the solitaire is from my first marriage, the two small diamonds are from my second, and the six small ones belong to this marriage, to Tom. They are inseparable."*

❋❋❋

An elderly couple gave a party to celebrate their fourth anniversary. It came about the same time that each of them would have been married to their original partners for 50 years, if those partners had lived. So they had this party and invited all their friends, both old and new, and they had a big cake that said: "Bill and Kay, 50 years; Ted and Lil, 50; Kay and Ted, 4."

Many couples seasoned by the experiences of their former relationships have learned that marrying again doesn't invalidate the love for a former mate; indeed, it can be a tribute to what went before — to what was learned, to what was given and received. Elin Schoen, author of *Widower*, writes this after her father, Bud, remarried, this time to a woman named Gloria.

"The truth of the matter is that Gloria's recognition of Bud's loss, her respect for it, her refusal to deny it — and my father's acceptance of her first husband as a cherished part not only of Gloria's past but of her entire being — form the cornerstone of their new marriage, the reason it is working. They talk freely of their earlier spouses. They share their memories. They do not look for their lost loves in each other."

XII

WITH WHAT MEASURE?

WANTED: Tall, independent white male, mid-sixties, seeks woman who enjoys new challenges, new ideas. Object: friendship or...?

♀ *"I used to take life seriously: 'Love is everything,' and all that. I've changed. I like bohemians."*

♀ *"I'm more particular now. There was one man who invited me to lunch. I declined, because he was short, nervous and high strung — the kind you'd have to take care of."*

♀ *"We have friends who lowered their standards because they were desperate. We didn't. Neither of us felt we had to have someone."*

♂ *"My standards are higher now, because the longer I live the more women there are!"*

♂ *"We'd have to love the same things...7-Up and cheese in the morning."*

In *Passages* Gail Sheehey says: "Middle age is definitely a time to have a healthy respect for eccentricity. This is only possible when we overcome the habit of trying to please everyone, which seems to be a late development for many women."

> **WANTED: Active, attractive man, past 50, to share life's pleasures with trim, active woman. No football watchers/beer drinkers, please!**

♀ *"I want a tall, nice-looking younger man with lots of hair and his own teeth. Someone lively. My first husband was bald and his main exercise was getting up to change the TV channel. That ended when we got remote control."*

♂ *"I've always felt inferior toward beautiful women, but that's never stopped me! I'm more confident now; the odds are in my favor."*

♂ *"I wouldn't be interested in a woman unless she has good ankles and good legs...that hasn't changed!"*

♂ *"I go for younger women because women my own age for the most part have let themselves slip. Maybe they're tired of making the effort to keep themselves up, to compete. I'm not attracted to fat women, so that rules out a lot of the older women I meet."*

♀ *"When you're young, you have time to take off the rough edges, you learn to smooth out irritations. That's more difficult when you're older and have been alone."*

> **WANTED: Female college grad, still a student of life at 70, wants to meet decisive, smart man for walks, conversation. Booklovers especially welcome.**

♀ *"One man asked me out. I said no. I didn't like him; I can't tell you why. In some ways he wasn't good enough. Not intellectual. Another old fool tried to kiss me. He was about 80. I didn't like his looks, or his grammar."*

"I WANT A MAN ... WITH
HIS OWN TEETH"

♂ *"I'm looking for mutual background, mutual interests. Intelligence. But I'd be frightened of a very bright woman. That hasn't changed. I've always preached you should marry the girl on your block."*

♀ *"I'm very fussy, always have been. Most men I meet now are dull, don't know how to talk to women. Also, I'm spoiled by tall men. There's one thing I would like: someone to make decisions for me. But most of them wouldn't make the decisions I'd want them to."*

♂ *"My standards have changed a lot. I accept women now as I accept men. Looks used to be all-important but now ideas matter more. Conversation is vital to me. I hate having to work at thinking of things to say."*

WANTED: Senior citizen, female, seeks man to share interests. Must be active Christian or looking for spiritual basis to life. No cultists.

♀ *"I have lived with my religion for many years. It's the last bit of identity I would let go of."*

♂ *"I have no problem with any type of religion. I'd make room for hers."*

♂ *"Our major concern right now is where to get married; we'd like it to be in a church we would continue to attend. As we search, we're finding out new things about each other."*

♂ *"I'm an active Christian Scientist, as my first wife was. One of our joys was reading the daily lesson together. Now? I don't know. When I was involved with someone who wasn't a Scientist, I really missed that sharing."*

♀ *"He'd have to believe in himself and in God. He'd be successful because he would have believed all his life."*

WANTED: Domestically-inclined male, age 65, is looking for female of like persuasion to share home and declining years.

♂ *"I've had 10 women in my home for dinner at different times, something I never did before my first marriage. Only three of those 10 offered to help with the dishes. If they were interested in me as a person, they might have offered."*

NO TIME LIKE THE PRESENT

"I admire your independence. And it's driving me crazy."

The speaker, a man in his sixties, is expressing a common conflict to his lady friend: a conflict between the desire to embrace today's concept of male/female relationships and the desire to maintain his traditional standards.

Some of us approach this conflict, and our changed personal needs, with optimism and humor.

♀ *"He gets mad at me but doesn't talk about leaving. That's impressed me more than anything. When I was younger, I'd have welcomed the challenge, maybe left him, just to show him."*
♂ *"I want to love someone enough so I'm willing to assume long-range responsibility for her even after my death. That wasn't the kind of thing I used to think about."*

For others, problems continue to abound. For example, the older woman who has given up her dream of finding — being found by — a "masculine," physically attractive man.

Her unfavorable position in the male/female ratio leads her to settle for any man. But has she really settled for this — in her heart? Once assured of security, she may come to resent the choice she made and take out her frustrations on him.

She may still be able to adjust her expectations, and some do. It is just as hard for a man. Relationships are different from those he enjoyed when he was young. Then, life was full of potential, crowded with people. Now he may be alone, trying to deal with a limited outlook, a life complicated by thwarted ambition or a sense of lost opportunities. This can affect his choice of a partner.

As one man expressed it: "It's like trying to force the wrong piece into a jigsaw puzzle. I'm so lonely that I try to make the other person fit into my carried-over image of what I'd like her to be."

It surprised me to learn that many older men and women are unwilling to work hard for a new relationship:

♂ *"If you feel your choices are limited, you're more likely to relax your standards than to abandon them. You may feel you shouldn't be doing this, making this match, but it's too much work to start over."*

♀ *"I asked myself why I was so willing to accept him at first, warts and all — something I wouldn't have done when I was younger. The truth is I felt I wouldn't have another chance. And of course it was good in some ways. I just didn't have the energy to look for anything better."*

OF RIGHT AND WRONG

Standards?

"If the right person came along all the standards I have set would fall by the wayside."

Pressed for a definition of "right," this 70-year-old man fell back on instinct: "I'll know her when I meet her."

Perhaps he should meet the woman who said: "I want to be married! I don't know any other way of life. But not just anybody, nothing's worth that; it would be all wrong. I'll keep looking. I'll find him!"

SUMMING UP

XIII

CLOSING STATEMENT BY THE PROSECUTION IN THE CASE OF A. LONE vs. WILL GOFORIT

Ladies and gentlemen of the jury: Witness after witness, all over the age of 60, have spoken eloquently about the difficulty and the pain they experience when they open their lives to someone of the opposite sex. Testifying for A. Lone, they have provided ample proof that the differences between them are more marked and more difficult to resolve now than they would have been 30 or 40 years ago.

Let me tell you, also, about the woman who said: "He's ready to retire; to travel, write, paint. I want to go back to school, get my master's. He says he's not able to be enthusiastic about the future, to plan for it, as I am. This problem — our arguments about it — are exhausting me."

Do you remember hearing about "little resentments"? One witness said that they crop up on a day-to-day basis. "We're not aware of them when we're young, perhaps because we mutter about them now instead of sounding off, as we would have 30 years ago. These things snowball into one big resentment."

I submit to you, ladies and gentlemen, that the attempts of those witnesses to make adjustments that will resolve these problems, ease the pain, often fall short. I give you the 68-year-old social worker who wanted to get married, while her gentlemen friend did not. What did she do?

"I have had to adjust to the limits of the relationship," she said, "and that has been painful. I spend more time at my own house now; I go to his only when it's convenient. I had thought for years that I wanted to marry him and it's been hard to let go. He resents my working when I could have retired. He gets angry about my 'getting into people's heads.' He swore when we met, 10 years ago, that he was too old to ever get married again. I guess he meant it."

Then there are both men and women who had been enjoying their single lives — a "trouble-free existence," as one witness called it. Then they found themselves entangled in a relationship, or in a marriage, and what happened? One said; "I enjoyed bachelorhood, with no one to boss me around. My new wife is old enough to have a certain set of mind. She can be impatient and intolerant, critical. My entire existence is now exposed to advice."

Pain. Disappointment. Resentment. We have proved our point over and over.

The defense has contended that a balance can be struck, a balance between long-established, contrasting life styles. My learned opponent even tried to promote the idea that partners can contribute to each other through their differences! But I'm certain you'll understand the prosecution witness who spoke with such emotion about her diminished ability to control her environment after she started dating her 70-year-old friend. Whether it was the heat coming out of the furnace (he liked it cooler) or the cool colors she liked to have around her (he was partial to red) they were at odds. And the elderly gentleman who complained bitterly that he had so few choices as he approached his 80th birthday. He concluded that self-assertion, attempts to change to meet his new wife's demands, were useless. In the face of so much clear-cut testimony, can you believe that change is possible for these older citizens — as individuals, or as couples? Attorneys for the defense told you that it is, while again and again prosecution witnesses reported that change has become difficult, if not impossible!

Wayne Lavengood, MSW, a geriatric social worker, has testified: "Aging involves many different kinds of losses, including loss of control over life decisions. This can lead to depression. We tend to get into certain habits and the longer we have them, the more comfortable they are for us. We may not be willing to compromise. Another problem is deciding how to spend time together. It's less structured when you're older. Also, different degrees of sociability, long practiced, present a problem."

Another of our expert witnesses was struck by the number of older men and women who seek to avoid the pain of human relationships by adopting a pet. He said: "Loneliness may be better than learning to adapt to someone else. Here, in this town, many men and women have dogs or cats — a living entity — which substitutes for that need to learn to adapt."

Some substitute! You may ask why differences and similarities are more important in later years than in younger relationships. Let me suggest one reason: young people get some of their satisfactions elsewhere — in their jobs, for instance. Or from their children. Differences get magnified when you are together more, as you are in older years. One woman testified that she had been independent for 15 years before she married again. She had to leave the area where she had lived among family and friends all her life and was forced to find friends of her own as well as to try to fit into her new husband's circle, long-established. How traumatic that had been, for she spoke to you as a woman newly separated from that second husband.

You may be wondering why she didn't seek counseling. I'll tell you: older couples resist seeking advice because they think they already know it all. Also, their upbringing did not include constant exhortations by friends and by Ann Landers to "get professional help" — advice so freely offered today.

Yes, the times they are a-changin', my friends. What complicates matters is that it's all new territory for our older men and women — especially today's concept of macho men who are *also* gifted with sensitivity. We're in a transitional stage of male-female relationships. Men and women who grew up in one cultural environment are now living in another.

The complications extend to grown children, who, as one witness testified, "can reject you as a 'suitor' for their mother, make innuendos, put you down."

That witness also said that his women friends are often unavailable because they want to do things with their grown children, or with their own women friends. He told us: "What is frustrating for me is that older women seem more impressed with their women friends as companions. They only want a man if they are going out at night, or to make a pair for a dinner party. One woman said she finds other women more interesting than men, who often turn to golf and other 'dull' interests. Also, it may be that women no longer want to make the effort to relate to men. They don't want to fuss with clothes, makeup, etc. They may not want to bother with sex, either."

The defense has attempted to lighten these problems by injecting humor into these unfortunate situations. My learned opponent tried to minimize the problem of adjustments by producing a witness who claimed her biggest problem was that her new husband never folded his towels in thirds, as she had done all her life. Her husband's retort, right in this courtroom, was: "But look what *you* do — you drink out of the milk carton!"

Laughable? Perhaps. Another defense witness said, "I'm not watching as much TV. And I'm trying to teach her to ski." And another, that her biggest adjustment in a late marriage was "having someone around a lot when I'm used to working alone in my kitchen."

That last witness also said: "We're beyond money and children problems. One problem we do have is getting our names and addresses straightened out."

I remind you of these sad attempts to minimize the problems we are concerned about, only to counter them with the testimony of many witnesses to the opposite — to their pain, their frustration, their mental anguish, as evidenced by statements like these:

"You get selfish living by yourself. I'd hate to give that up."

"It can be rough! He has been a chef for years and I'm a good cook. It was strange for me not to be able to do anything right in the kitchen. I also objected to sharing the same bed with him that he had shared with his first wife."

"I feel that he doesn't have any absolutes, and I do . He's a minister, so I find that hard to understand. I think he is trying to make up for all the years in an unhappy marriage and that I can't count on him being faithful to me. I've decided I just have to get over him as best I can, and hope I meet someone else."

"My husband is in a convalescent home. I go to see him three times every week. He's resigned to living there and wants me to live there too. But I'm not ready for it. I find strong support in my present environment, a retirement complex where I have friends and there are clubs, entertainment."

In conclusion, ladies and gentlemen of the jury, we have proven conclusively that relationships between older men and older women result in pain and mental anguish, that these men and women would be better off living apart.

Now I want to leave you with just one more piece of testimony in favor of my client, A. Lone — the experience of a couple in their seventies. And I will ask you to consider whether any of you, ladies and gentlemen of the jury, would want to be this man or this woman.

"I was divorced for eight years. There was an older man across the street. Both of us were very active. We started dating. After a while he asked, 'Why don't we get married?'

Our families were delighted. We did get married and I moved across the street to his house. I kept mine, too.

"He didn't want me to move even an ashtray in his house. ('That's where *she* kept it,' he would say.) I left the garage door open. He blew his top and told me 'We always closed the door.'

"I moved back to own house and got an annulment. We still see each other, talk, are somewhat friendly. But it has been the most painful experience in my life."

XIV

CLOSING STATEMENT BY THE DEFENSE IN THE CASE OF A. LONE vs. WILL GOFORIT

We have heard a compelling case by the prosecution. You have heard my colleague's contention that his client, A. Lone, and many other senior citizens have worked hard to attain life styles that bring them satisfaction, and peace. His client, on the stand and under oath, admitted that at times he was tempted to admit someone into the intimacy of his life. He further stated, however, that he preferred the lifestyle he had worked so hard to build. He listed ways in which he has learned to cope with being alone. Perhaps you detected, members of the jury, as I did, a certain defensiveness in his position. The gentleman doth protest too much, methinks!

I now submit to you that the defense has proved — beyond any doubt — that "letting someone in" can open the door to happiness, and to mental and physical health. We do not ignore the risks involved. You heard my client, Will Goforit, admit them. But Will — and the stream of witnesses who followed him — clearly stated that the joys of being involved in relationships far outweigh those risks.

One witness spoke of his new relationship as "a lovely blending together of two long lives." He was followed on the stand by his wife of two years. Hear her testimony:

"Sharing experiences is the best thing about it. You appreciate sunsets more and it's wonderful to share them. I had forgotten how nice it is to share. We have so much in common: I feel as though I have known him forever."

The strength of my client's position was also evident in the cross-examination of a prosecution witness. "I never minded the days alone," one elderly woman said. But when pressed, she continued: "Well, yes, I might feel rotten in the middle of the night or hear spooks and I didn't have anyone to turn to." There was no mistaking the warmth of her smile when she added, "Now I do" — before the prosecutor could object.

What is so good, so healthful, about relationships between older men and women? Our defense witnesses put it in different words, but the message was the same:

"Each day we do the things we want to do. We can afford to now, and are free to. We don't feel our age!"
"We are content to be together and to be home. No longer are we looking for a lot of excitement."
"The companionship is the greatest pleasure. I had learned that I can be alone, but I like the extra intimacy. It works for us because I'm easy to get along with, and he's a nice guy."
"At this age we have the freedom to say what we want frankly and that cements the relationship."

"We both enjoy traveling and neither of us enjoyed traveling alone. We enjoy being together and now we have more time for it."

"A special joy for me is having the companionship of a partner for dinner and to go places you don't go with other women."

"There's lots to talk about! And we can use all our previous experience at relating and living with someone, whether it was good or bad. We have more time to spend together every day. This relationship may be all the more wonderful because neither of us expected it."

"It's nice not to have to worry about getting pregnant. And I like having someone make decisions for me."

Did it register with you, ladies and gentlemen of the jury, how often that word "companionship" came into the testimony of the defense witnesses? Hear these words too:

"The greatest pleasure, now, with a man, would be companionship. The fun of enjoying the same things together. It doesn't have to be elegant. Just being in each other's company."

"I'd love a companion who likes to go places and do things. I'm 82 and I love to travel, go to concerts, art shows, movies, plays. Dancing! I'd love to start dancing again! And to have someone to entertain with. I don't like to go places by myself; it's not safe to go out at night alone."

And the word "sharing":

"What would be special about a relationship now? Sharing with someone. Even just when buying a pretty dress:

without someone to show it to, I sometimes take it back. Having someone meet me at the airport when I come home from a trip. Or having someone share the trip!"

✳✳✳

The prosecution would have us think that Will Goforit and like thinkers are selfish, concerned only with their own comfort and well-being. Not so! Hear the testimony of one woman:

"I would like to have that feeling of really caring for one person, for a man. Even if I were to be hurt. To be hurt is being alive."

So much for the prosecution's contentions regarding the pains of involvement.

✳✳✳

Many of the defense witnesses testified that mature relationships are not just as good as younger ones — they are better! Let me tell you of some of their testimony; I exhort you to remember it convincingly when you go into the jury room in a few minutes.

"One friend described me as 'glowing from the inside' after I met my second husband. We both had an amazing amount of energy because we were so in love. Companionship wasn't enough for us; love is not overlooked in later marriages, as some think. And I got two instant grandchildren!"

"One's habits and personal traits and idiosyncrasies are more obvious now, and one sees the other's more clearly too. I didn't see them as an adolescent. We were buffeted by wars and depressions early. Now I'm better able to manage my emotions; age has given me more stability in that department. Now that I see patterns more clearly, I can do something about them. I can ignore more and forgive more."

"With maturity, you know you don't own anybody. I think I'm more mellow than I used to be; everything is not as important as it used to be. My values have changed. I'm better at respecting another person's wants and desires. I don't use people any more."

"He's making it possible for me to grow, without restriction. And we have a wonderful sense of living from moment to moment."

"I'd never want to live alone again. There is an ease about my life now. No possessive attitude, no demands. It's nice to have the consideration of someone else and the thoughtfulness, and to be able to return that, without expecting anything back. You don't have to take all the events of the day too seriously...live and let live. The little things that young people get irritated about don't bother us. When younger, we demanded more of each other and there was a lot of pressure to 'keep up with the Joneses.' This is a more rational type of relationship. I can't imagine life without him. We have become comfortable; we balance one another. We're good for each other."

"My wife had been a widow for about a year when we married. She became a different woman — joyful! Now we have a feeling of freedom, a lack of restraint I didn't have in my first marriage. We recognized in each other the values each had acquired over the years."

"I now have time for my friends and I can do things for them. I can work out relationship problems better; I know how to set limitations for myself. When I get tired, I stop."

"At a time when children are leaving the nest for good I don't have to feel that I must depend on them. I can let them go."

❊❊❊

The prosecution made much of the differences, so long-lived, between older men and older women. We contend — and have proved — that these differences can be an important plus in keeping up energy and interests...to any age.

The prosecution has called to your attention the changing times. We have no argument with the fact that times are changing. We do contend, however, that this adds further strength to the case of Will Goforit. As one witness said:

"My fantasy of fulfillment now is to have a woman companion, rent a van and take off — go where we want. Leave it all behind. Death is final; you don't need to suffer up to it. I'm more free now of cultural, family and social pressures."

And another:

"The times have helped us. We have carried over the gains women made in the 60's, which freed me from having to be any man's shadow."

The prosecution cited experts in support of A. Lone's case. We also cite experts. The same social worker who testified about loss and depression, Wayne Lavengood, also said, "Time takes on a different perspective. People can enjoy things they didn't have time for before. Trips, walks on the beach. There's more room for sharing without the demands of work, kids. And for sharing memories...because they have more!"

We also cite another kind of expert...authors, who bring us the important evidence of the heart.

Anne Morrow Lindberg: *Bring Me a Unicorn*: "Mrs. Neilson (wife of the president of Smith College) said how nice it was when one was married and old. One could show people just how much one liked them without complications following."

Daisy Newman: *Indian Summer of the Heart*: (Serenity speaks) "Taking risks is leaving the outcome to God...I think it's even more wonderful for old people, who know how rough life can be, sometimes, to make this commitment." (Oliver says to himself) "We may not have many years...But love isn't measured by time. It may be the only thing in the universe that lives forever."

Arry (a character in the play *Morning's at Seven*, by Paul Osborn): "What does it mean to you to grow old, Thor?...Doesn't getting old mean that — well, that things don't trouble you so much any more? That everything's peaceful and quiet..."
Thor (once, many years ago, her lover): "Peaceful and quiet! I guess that must be when you get *real* old, Arry, say in your late eighties."

Arry: "I always thought of getting old sort of like when you're nice and drowsy — and yet you know you won't fall asleep for a little while yet — and you just lie there sort of comfortably — and enjoy it. But it isn't that way at all...I guess it's nice and peaceful if you got a home. If you got a husband. If you got somebody to get old with. But I haven't."

There, indeed, is the pain that A. Lone and other prosecution witnesses testified to. But there is also the remedy for that pain. We can agree that the risks in a relationship with someone of the opposite sex are greater when you are older. But so, my friends, are the joys — far greater! I feel certain that you will carry that conviction with you into the jury room.

I thank you.

✼✼✼

Two gray-haired jurors walk from the courthouse together. One, a man, says to the other, a woman:

"Well, that's over! I'm glad it turned out the way it did. For a moment there I was afraid..."

He put his hand on her arm.

"I've been thinking that I'd like to know you better, away from all this. What do you say...shall we plan a picnic, go to the beach together?"

The woman hesitates. Then she smiles.

"Well, all right...yes, I'd like that!"

✼✼✼